CHANGING STEP

* * * * * * * * * *

THE AUTOBIOGRAPHY OF JILL BEATTY

CHRISTIAN FOCUS PUBLICATIONS

Published by
Christian Focus Publications Ltd.
Geanies House, Fearn,Ross-shire,
IV20 1TW, GREAT BRITAIN
Printed in Great Britain
by Cox & Wyman Ltd, Reading

I SBN 1 871 676 681

CONTENTS

In memory of
Rex
my beloved husband

FOREWORD

What an exciting life Jill has lived.

A young vivacious opportunist, she looked for and most certainly found thrilling adventures in many lands.

Crouching in an air-raid shelter in the London Blitz was but the beginning. This energetic Physical Education teacher joned the army, and in the Middle East in those turbulent and horror-filled war years narrowly escaped death on several occasions.

With many a male escort she plunged headlong into a fun-loving round of pleasure, being reprimanded by her superiors on one occasion for dancing on the tables of a Cairo Hotel. Such things Army Officers ought not to do!

She is so frank and honest that it is real and living.

Her talents and dedication were recognised by the authorities and she was honoured with the award of 'Mentioned in Dispatches' for distinguished service.

Then she met Rex; manly, strong, gentlemanly, disciplined, tender Rex; Rex, the much decorated and highly respected army officer; Rex the son of a surgeon who was a missionary in China. With the war over they married and settled in Britain.

Rex's early Christian upbringing worked its way through and he returned to a true and living faith. For Jill that came so slowly, yet at last she too found the Saviour her husband was now preaching. He entered the ministry of the Church of Scotland and she became the lady of the manse.

The story of her beautiful teenage daughter's brain haemorrhage, the subsequent partial recovery and pleasant, loving relationship is told with touching pathos.

The heartache of an evangelical minister who preaches the gospel to a congregation which largely does not know or value the biblical truths of salvation is clearly depicted and keenly felt by the reader.

Then came Rex's last great battle; this time with cancer - and here Jill's heart is exposed. Yet the depth of her sorrow is translated into ministry to others. This speaks to your heart. Who will forget the scene of father and son clutching one another in a last tearful embrace; or of Jill sobbing in the park? We can but learn from one who has walked the path of sorrow, who has gathered herself together and who has begun to build a new life once again. God gives 'beauty for ashes, the oil of joy for mourning, the garment of praise for the spirit of heaviness' (Is. 61:3).

One picture is etched indelibly on my mind. Rex was in the Hospice and had but a few days to live. Seeing other visitors approach his bed, I said my goodbyes and withdrew. Near the door I turned to wave, but he had just become aware of the new arrivals, and lifted his arm to these Christian friends in a greeting. At that moment the Glory of God descended upon him. His face lit up with a glorious, heavenly light. I saw it, I stood at the door and gazed, and worshipped, and wept. I weep now as I write. The moment was divine. I had never seen anything like it, nor have I since. It is a moment that I will treasure till I die. Next Sunday morning in Hollyrood Abbey I heard Rev. James Philip say, 'This week I watched a saint of God pass on to glory.' Yes Jim, and so did I.

Jill, your book ministers. It ministers to the careless who are outside of Christ, to those who need strength to cope with handicapped loved ones, to the confused who are learning slowly and need encouragement, to those who proclaim the precious biblical message of a living Saviour in an environment of apathy and mistrust, and to the bereaved and brokenhearted who need a Comforter. You have found him abundantly able to succour and satisfy the deepest needs of your heart in so many of life's experiences. May those who read this book be likewise led to this wonderful Saviour.

I count it a privilege to have written these few words.

Rev. Colin N Peckham B.A. M.th.
Principal,
Faith Mission Bible College,
Edinburgh.

Aqaba, Jordan 1945

We sat in a circle, cross-legged on the floor. Before us sat a great round dish. We peered forward tentatively to discover its contents. Nobody wanted to imagine too vividly what this enormous container held and what, it appeared, we were expected to eat.

We sat in a large, dark hut and around us was an unusual assortment of people. The hut was the home of the Muktah, the Arab village head-man, who had invited us to join him for a meal. This friendly gesture had also been extended to various other men from the village and they squatted beside us, watching carefully to examine these British army officers at close quarters. With me were several friends, all enjoying a few precious days away from the army routine and the discipline of the Garrison at Sarafand in Palestine.

A party of us were visiting Aqaba, which is in the southern-most part of Jordan, travelling in jeeps over the rough, sandy ground. It was a delightful time, camping on the shores of the Gulf and spearing fish in the dark nights by the light of lanterns which we carried. The lights would reflect softly off the gently lapping water. The slow progress of those nights was a welcome change from the scorching heat and busy clamour of the days when the earth-shaking bombs, the roaring aircrafts and the constant staccato rifle fire crowded our ears.

Great clouds of steam rose from the dish. Within the basic ingredient appeared to be rice but chunks of meat and various other mysterious items were visible. As we watched peculiar bits and pieces 'plopped' into the food from the straw roof above! We knew not to expect utensils and were quickly shown how to take a handful, form the food into a roll and eat it. As a special favour I was offered the eye of a sheep! The thought of eating this horrified me. It stared balefully up at me, slimy and wet. I shuddered and quickly concealed it in my hand. Behind my back I frantically tried to pass it to my neighbour, to get rid of it without causing offence: to offend an Arab could indeed be a dangerous act.

Smuggling the food away around the circle I thought of myself as a child and murmured, 'How like home all this is.' My brothers had been marvellously adept at disposing of whatever food I disliked without arousing my father's suspicions. I have always disliked fat on meat and blancmanges have similarly been able to turn my stomach on sight, but I was always made to sit until I ate my food. At home we had a large, heavily carved dining-room table with a broad shelf underneath it. When my meat was fatty I would put my handkerchief on my lap, push the fat off the plate on to it and hide it on the ledge. Later we would smuggle it outside and throw it away. Such deceit the rigid discipline of home produced. Then, I did not know the much stricter discipline of the Army and service in the Middle East awaited me, and that occasionally I would employ much more daring deception whenever it suited me to avoid it.

1
Growing Up

As a child I lived with my family in the West End of London. Due to my father's job as a chauffeur we also spent three months of every year in the village of Corfe Castle in Dorset. Being born in 1916, during the First World War, it was indeed much safer to live in the country than in the capital and our time in Corfe was often extended. In those early years, and thereafter, my three brothers and I had such fun climbing trees and leading healthy, outdoor lives. An unashamed tomboy, I would follow my three brothers in all that they would do.

My parents were loving and hard-working, my mother small and endearing. My mother's aspect was one of contentment and concern for her family and my father, its head. He was an army man having been in the Royal Flying Corps, and he had also fought in the Boer War in South Africa but had returned with a form of Parkinson's disease and was considered unfit for many kinds of employment. It was perhaps his training in the services which had instilled in him a strong sense of discipline. We were most certainly brought up according to the Biblical principle, 'Spare the rod and spoil the child!' If my father spoke, we obeyed. Bad language was never heard nor was alcoholic drink ever seen in the house.

As we grew up, difficult and hard times surrounded everybody. The Great War was closely followed by the Depression, the General Strike and widespread unemployment. In those early days of my youth I cannot remember the deepest anxieties of my parents, but I do remember quite often seeing my dear little mother weeping quietly. She was tiny - just 5' 2' beside my father, stiff and erect and a whole foot taller than her!

Schools were also places of strict discipline. Immediate obedience was required, otherwise a sharp ruler was used by the teacher. I was allowed to go to the village school in Dorset with my two older brothers when I was three. Wallace, or 'Dod' as he was affectionately known, and Jack were supposed to take care of me but I soon considered that I should take care of them! One day Jack was going to be smacked by the teacher in front of the class. I stood on my chair shouting, 'You will not smack him! You will not!' and so disrupted the discipline of the class. I was not allowed to return until I was a little older - my rebelliousness began at an early age!

We were also sent to church on Sundays. My brothers, even Joseph, the youngest, wore caps, naturally taking them off in church. I did not wear a hat. The vicar was so shocked at this arrogant little girl of five from London not covering her head in God's house that he took one of my brothers' caps and put it on my head. Immediately I snatched it off, and have never forgotten this incident.

As we grew older we stayed in London for the whole year. Fond memories remain, however, of a thatched cottage in Corfe even though it had afforded few luxuries. There had been no electricity - oil lamps and candles had provided our light - nor was there a bathroom. Once a week the tin hip-bath was put before the fire and we were all well scrubbed. Similarly, the only 'loo' was at the bottom of the garden. Our childish hearts would sink when my father was seen disappearing down the garden with the newspaper. It meant a long wait.

Returning to London permanently, we soon discovered that the great city provided plenty of scope for four naughty mischief-makers. As in Dorset, we were all sent to Sunday School. On the Sunday morning we were given a penny each for the collection. Quite frequently however we did not arrive at class and used the pennies for bus fares and visited any museum or amusement which might be open.

Fun-loving and encouraging each other to naughtiness, the four of us would be sent off to amuse ourselves and keep out of the way. We lived within walking distance of Oxford Street which buzzed with activity. At an early age I was taught to contain fear as my brothers dared me to do things. If I refused they called me a coward which was more than I could bear. When the first escalator appeared at Selfridges, the largest store in Oxford Street, they dared me to run up the 'down' escalator. This, of course, I did but was forcibly turned out of the shop.

Naturally we went in again by another door!

Soon Belisha beacons were introduced on to the London streets. They had large orange bowls on top of black and white striped poles, and marked places where pedestrians could cross. We quickly acquired a broom handle which we painted black and white and on the top we fixed an orange balloon. This we took around with us, putting it on the kerbside and crossing the road wherever we liked. We found this hilarious but the police were not quite so amused!

During the early thirties my father obtained employment as a verger at an Anglo-Catholic church. We continued to live in central London and the accommodation which was provided was quite close to Paddington Station. To us as children, the church was very strange - the priests were called 'father' and wore funny hats. We were told to bob up and down as we went into the pews and whenever we faced the altar. So many times we were reminded to make the sign of the cross. We would giggle and stumble over each other as we rushed in.

Inside the church were large pictures of Jesus' journey to Calvary. The pictures were called the 'Stations of the Cross' and the priest would carry a pot of incense towards each picture. My brother Jack, was much more interested in all the ceremony and rituals of the church than I was. At the age of twelve he became a Censer, which involved him processing in robes through the church. We would tease him about his lacy white surplice which he wore, but Jack is still very interested in the church and the ritual attached to the High Church. He was also much more academic than the rest of us and eventually became the Lord Mayor of Westminster following his war-time service in Bomber Command.

I was confirmed in this church when I was eleven. Dressed in white and wearing a veil, I read a long list of confessions from a prepared card. I am sure it had been impressed upon me what it all meant but I remained in the dark and was unaffected by the whole proceedings.

Unless financial facilities were available, educational opportunities during the years of the Depression were not considered very important, especially for girls. I, however, was much more interested in gymnastics and games than in book-learning and my ambition then was to be a Physical Education teacher. My elder brothers both left school for work - 'Dod' trained as an electrician and Jack became a skilled draughtsman. Not to be outdone, I, who had followed my brothers in everything also left school determined to earn my living. I was 14 and thought myself rich earning 14/- a week. My determination to teach Physical Education did not diminish however and I began attending all the evening classes I possibly could to improve my ability for Physical activities. I even trained as a Greek ballet dancer! Soon I gained parts, dancing in cabarets on the stage of London's Palladium and at the Royal Albert Hall in the chorus of *Haiawatha*.

During this time I began to rebel against the authority enforced upon me by my father, but always secretly, for fear of punishment. I would sneak downstairs and slip out to be with my brothers and their friends, putting on my make-up and removing my thick stockings (which I was forced to wear) as soon as I was out of sight! I felt no guilt about my deceit but only thought that I deserved a good time.

In central London was the London County Council College for Physical Training. A three year course which could be completed in the evenings was offered. Desperate to apply, the moment I was eighteen I attended the necessary tests and exams, but failed. Such is the optimism of youth that I had never even considered failure. I cried and cried and was terribly disappointed. Being young and resilient however, I bounced back into activities. I soon joined the Central Council of Physical Recreation (CCPR) and became a member of the British team.

In 1938, I was 22 and part of the team due to represent Britain in Germany at the Hamburg Rally. As the fear of war with Germany was very strong, many were unsure of the wisdom of going. My employers particularly requested that I withdraw. I, however, had my head full of travel and adventure and had no care for world affairs or politics. I was delighted when it was decided that the plan would go ahead. Germany sent their beautiful liner, *The Bremen*, to collect us. Because of the expected Declaration of War and the lack of enthusiasm for our participation, we were taken in tenders outside the three-mile limit off Southampton waters and were piped aboard out at sea!

We marched before Hitler. Security was very tight and never at any time were we allowed to wander about by ourselves. We were always accompanied by numerous 'brownshirts', even into shops. Demonstrations of rhythmic exercises and dancing with skipping ropes were given each day. Forty countries were gathered and we all were accommodated on Germany's cruising liner, *Gunstoff Willheim*. Various members of the Nazi Party dined with the teams each evening.

On the final evening we were taken to the side of a lake and witnessed a ballet being danced on an island in the middle of it. As a grand finale, cannons fired all the flags of the represented countries into the air and the flags fell on to the water. Lastly, the flags of Germany - the Swastikas - were fired and all these landed on top of the other countries'! The 'brownshirts,' later to be the SS, prompted us to give the Nazi salute. Only as I look back is it possible to see why so many in this country were against any British team attending this 'Strength through Joy' rally in 1938.

This experience helped me considerably in my determination to fulfill my ambitions, and on my next application to the Physical Education College I was accepted and eventually became a qualified teacher.

Back home, my mother was very ill. She had taken a stroke some time previously but we had managed to nurse her at home. My father gave her his devoted attention. He remained dictatorial to those of us at home but tended to my mother with much gentleness and love. At nights he would refuse to sleep beside her for fear of disturbing her and for eighteen months slept on a couch pulled near to her bed to be close at hand.

Just before war was declared my dear little mother had a massive stroke. Having been out for a short trip that day she appeared to be very tired when suddenly we knew that something was very wrong.

'Take her upstairs,' barked my father.

'We can't,' I cried, somehow realising that this was much more serious than before.

This was the first time I had ever defied my father and not followed his command. He stared, not in anger, but suddenly lost and uncertain, unable to turn to my quiet, gentle mother upon whom he, and the rest of us depended so heavily.

Like a little boy, he pleaded, 'Well, where can we take her?' his voice unnaturally quiet.

'To hospital,' I replied and proceeded to take charge of the situation.

From that moment on, I felt as if some change had come over me. I had broken free from obeying the rule of my father. I had disobeyed him, not under-handedly like before, not in hiding, but openly, asking him to respect my judgment. Even in the midst of it all, the trauma and suffering of my mother's subsequently brief illness, I felt changed. I could, and would rely on myself. I would follow my own heart.

My mother died as a result of this final stroke. Left alone, my father was broken and empty. Sitting silently at home he seemed unconscious of the family or our concern for him. Often it is only when someone close to us dies that we realise how much we have relied upon them. In my distress, I walked the busy streets, dejected and miserable, barely aware of the flurry of activity going on around me. For London was furiously busy. War had been declared. A war which lasted for six long years and left fifty million dead.

London was a hive of activity, with sandbags everywhere. Gas masks were distributed and air-raid shelters erected. For a while we were all waiting, waiting and nothing happened for a year. During this time I was teaching at a school near Baker Street and on most evenings at a school in Wapping in the East End of London as fewer teachers were available, many leaving to join the Armed Services.

This waiting period dragged on and became known as the 'phoney war'. By the time it ended my three brothers had all volunteered for the services. 'Dod' and Joseph left for the Army and Jack became a navigator in the Airforce. My father also tried to join up but nobody would accept him, so I stayed in London with my father near Paddington Station and continued to teach until the blitz made it dangerous and impossible for classes to continue.

Strangely enough I did not worry about the raids but guiltily enjoyed the comradeship and excitement of it all. One night I was returning home by the Underground when a raid began. The stations were closed for the duration of the raid so all the passengers had to remain underground. I was perfectly safe but by the time I arrived home my poor father was so worried that he was angry with me for going at all!

Seven weeks of bombing followed and for those seven weeks I did not go to bed. Crouching in our air-raid shelter, sirens wailing and bombs exploding, sleep was impossible. During the day extreme fatigue would overcome me so that I would watch my hands shake with the tiredness. Even amongst all this, the morale in London remained high. One day when I was out after a night of air-raids, I saw a shop window which had been blown out. A large notice inside read, 'More open than usual!' Nothing could beat their bravery and indefatigable sense of humour.

Like so many families with sons away in the services, we lived in fear of receiving the dreaded telegram, 'The War Office regrets ..... . ' We could not remain exempt from grief for long and within a few months of his volunteering, news arrived that my youngest brother, Joseph, had been killed. He was only twenty-one. The Army gave us the choice of having the body sent home for either a private or military funeral. My father, grieving painfully, so soon after my mother's death, requested a private, family funeral and wished my brother's body to be buried alongside my mother's, his wife's.

My other brothers were away at war so I was to be responsible for collecting his coffin from the train and bringing it home. Meeting that train and fulfilling my unhappy task will remain with me as one of my most distressing experiences. By this time the bombing raids were occurring not only at nights but also during the day. As I headed towards King's Cross Station the London streets were in chaos. The fear of day-time bombing meant that it was barely possible to resume normal existence and the debris of bombing and subsequent fires was always visible.

I arrived to meet the evening train to find the whole station in darkness. Nameless people rushed around the platforms and over the lines. A raid had taken place earlier and chaos reigned. The station was open to the sky as the glass roof had been shattered and broken glass was everywhere, splintering dangerously underfoot in the poor light. Stumbling over rubble and debris and great heaps of broken glass I made my way to the train which held the coffins.

After what seemed like hours, shivering in the darkness I found to my distress that I had received the wrong coffin. In all the confusion, one little person looking for the body of her young brother did not mean much at all, and I waited miserably for hours before I was helped to correct this awful situation. On my way home, having again scrambled over the strewn evidence of destruction, I was in a state of misery and tears.

'Why are you crying?' my father asked.

I replied fiercely, 'Why indeed! Mummy died so recently and now Joseph is dead. Why shouldn't I cry?'

My father told me I had no faith! What did he mean? What faith? He had never spoken about faith before and how could faith alter the sadness surrounding me? I did not ask and my father did not try to explain. Every day there were so many deaths, and so many families were mourning the loss of loved ones from so many homes.

What was faith?

How could faith help?

2
Joining Up

Just as I had followed my brothers in leaving school, I soon longed to follow them into war-time service. Everyday existence had become wrapped up in the war and I wanted to be a part of the show; to join in and become 'one of the boys'. I was still too young to be conscripted but in my determination to be a part of the war effort, I decided to volunteer.

What horror was expressed when I announced this to the wider family. 'How wicked' I was - 'how selfish'. Not only did my father disapprove but my relatives totally condemned me for leaving him, a grieving, ailing widower. I did leave home, however, the clamour of protests not moving me from my decision.

Initially, I entered a female training centre in Lancaster, where every day hundreds were reporting for training. That day two hundred women arrived. They were an odd assortment from all areas of the country, although mainly from the north of England. Nearly all had been conscripted and were actually younger than me. They were also very rough: at least half of them had fleas, and even my experiences teaching in Wapping had not prepared me for their hardness and crudity.

On that first day, after the medical checks were completed we were allocated to huge dormitories with thirty to each room. Rough, iron bunk-beds lined the walls and we were issued our Army sleeping gear: three grey blankets, a lumpy pillow without a pillowcase and an Army 'biscuit'. These 'biscuits' were squares of rough material stuffed with straw which when joined in a row of three made a type of mattress. That first night and many thereafter were very uncomfortable.

On the following day we were issued with our first uniform and we queued for hours to receive painful innoculations. Although we were all now dressed alike, many of the women considered me to be different and indeed snobby. Perhaps I was. I was certainly resented because I had volunteered but I was also a teacher, and therefore a professional - and a Londoner. After the vaccination scars appeared, the roughest amongst our in-take would delight in punching me in the arm when our superiors were not looking. At first I would climb into my bunk at night and although I tried to sleep hot tears would sting my eyes. Staring up at the ceiling and hearing the heavy breathing of the women around me, I wondered what I had done. Too late though. It may be awful but what did I expect? The war was raging and I had volunteered. I could not go back!

Because I was a trained Physical Education teacher my promotion was swift and I soon became a sergeant. I was posted to Devises, in Wiltshire and took up my first responsibilities there. As well as being responsible for the Auxiliary Territorial Service (ATS) physical training, I was in charge of the girls in whose dormitory I slept. This was my first real experience of imposing rather than receiving discipline and I soon discovered the problems which this entailed. On one dreadful occasion I discovered that one of my girls had become pregnant and had indeed given birth, but the child was still-born. Everyone had kept silent and protected the girl from the punishment she would have received. The first I knew of it was when I discovered them trying to put the tiny dead baby down the lavatory!

I was quickly discovering that my experience of the world was very limited and my life had so far been more sheltered than I had been aware. I had never used bad language, had never smoked, had never taken an alcoholic drink. Now I was thrust into an environment where these habits and much worse were considered normal behaviour. I too, soon became 'one of the boys' in this mixed camp, adopting the habits of those around me and enjoying the cameraderie of the officers' mess where there were few female sergeants amongst many men.

From Wiltshire, I was moved to various training centres in the country, either being trained myself as a Junior Officer at Edinburgh's Redford Barracks, or training others in physical education as I did at Guildford in Surrey and later on the Isle of Man. Both Edinburgh and Guildford proved to be entirely female camps and perhaps this encouraged the more ladylike mode of living which I adopted. I could not remain a tomboy all my life.

In Guildford I became responsible for all new recruits. I had only been in the ATS myself for a few months and could remember well my own first fears and bewilderment on joining up. In that year there were 1,000 women in the camp, as new recruits were sent to us for their initial training. I had a team of Non-Commissioned Officers (NCOs) beneath me, all very good, hard-working and responsible women. I had to rely on them to help me maintain discipline as we trained and worked from early in the morning until late in the evening.

Just as we expected the girls under our command to obey orders so had we to obey the parade ground commands of the male sergeant major from the adjacent barracks. Every day we were drilled, irrespective of the weather or conditions. But morale was high even as the intensity of the war abroad increased. Even while the girls helped to 'man' the guns in the trenches in the dead of night, or were endlessly marched to and fro on the parade ground in the teeming, freezing rain, somehow they retained their enthusiasm and spirit.

It was during this time that I met up with some of my brothers' friends who had been part of a crowd of young folk I had known in London. Together we would go on outings when our free time coincided. I became particularly friendly with Denis who was an Officer in the Royal Artillery. He was tall and handsome and I enjoyed his hearty company. So much of my life was governed by my desire to 'try anything' and enjoy myself that I soon found myself engaged to Denis although I had given little thought to marriage. He was good fun and good looking and I liked him - hardly the most powerful reasons for agreeing to a proposal of marriage! Needless to say our engagement lasted only a few months until we were sent to new army posts.

My next posting was to the Isle of Man where I trained women in the 'Y' Service Signals. I also enjoyed the more relaxed lifestyle on the island. Being off the mainland we were much safer with fewer air raids and much less susceptible to bomb attacks. For this reason a number of the Officers were there to recuperate having received wounds while in the battlefields, and several were escapees from German Prisoner of War camps. In the mixed Officers' Mess we were regaled with exciting stories of the war zones and I began to crave the unpredictable and dangerous lifestyles which they described. I remember one soldier detailing his escape from imprisonment. He had curled up in a rubbish bin and was transported out of his camp by unsuspecting refuse collectors. He had inserted a small pipe into the lid of the bin so that he could breathe and thereby escaped - in broad daylight!

It was perhaps wrong of me to long for experiences which were so traumatic and life-threatening to my friends but at that time I was wrapped up in the adventure of it all and found Britain, and particularly the Isle of Man, very tame in comparison to what I knew was happening abroad. I soon decided that what I wanted to do more than anything was to volunteer for Overseas Service.

My life in the Isle of Man, however, was filled with social activities which I entered into with whole - hearted enthusiasm. Unlike the British Army on the mainland at this time, we were able to indulge in many cocktail parties and dances, taking every advantage of our relative safety a long way from the bombing. My drinking and smoking increased steadily as we drank many drinks at the bar before dinner and many more after when we were not on duty. But even then, I think I knew myself, amongst all the social activity, as a rather vulgar self - centred person - my life revolving around flirting with the other officers and holding my own with foul language and smutty stories. Bad habits always seem to be learned more quickly and successfully than good!

It was during this posting that I was expertly taught to play bridge. Four headmasters who served in the Education Corp would sit huddled over a square card table and play for hours on end. Their concentration and complicated money transactions intrigued me. When I asked to be taught, however, I was firmly told that I must sit silently and observe them for a whole month and if I still wanted to learn after this period then they would teach me. Having been set this challenge I determined to rise to it and after many weeks I began to become proficient at the game. It is perhaps a measure of my proficiency, however, that for all my practise, it never made me rich!

My application for Overseas Service was submitted in 1944 and I was recalled to the mainland to attend the required Army Overseas Service Board. My philosophy to all that was before me was 'try anything' - take what fun I could get, there was a war on! This daredevil attitude seemed to be acceptable and I passed the Overseas Board and was promoted to Captain a little later. I was going abroad. I did not know where but that was unimportant, I just wanted the next stage to start as quickly as possible.

Before long I was on the move, preparing for overseas duty. At all times our destination, even the next training camp, remained a mystery because of the importance of strict security. I did find myself in a camp in Wales, however, having been travelling overnight. There, with other officers I was kitted out with tropical equipment and we all received various travel permits and numerous vouchers before being shunted on again into the night.

The next day we found ourselves in Liverpool Docks, looking up at the most enormous liner. *The Georgic* had been commandeered for use by the forces but for all its great size it became vastly overcrowded as we all boarded. The ship was to carry 5,000 men and women from all parts of the army although it was only designed for 1,000. We were packed into every available space with sixteen officers to a cabin. The cramped conditions were much worse for the lower ranks but soon all 5,000 of us were provided with some corner on board and we were ready to sail - not one of us knowing where we were headed.

We soon discovered that at least we were bound for the Mediterranean as our first port of call was to be Naples. Here nobody was allowed to disembark and we could only look longingly across the harbour towards the city. We then sailed through the Straits of Messina, zig-zagging through turbulent seas, and on to Piraieus. Some of us longed to disembark to visit Athens and other places of interest, but we carried some troops who were under guard and a few had attempted to escape by jumping overboard so we headed out to sea again, the weather getting warmer and warmer.

Because the seas were heavily mined life-belts were worn at all times. We complained amongst ourselves - they were so uncomfortable as each day became progressively hotter. Throughout the trip we also had regular lifeboat drills but little other than the simplest duties were demanded of us. For the whole trip I played rubber after rubber of bridge. We played for high stakes and as the seas tossed the laden ship so did my fortune fluctuate. Although my winnings were occasionally high I finished our voyage with the accumulated wealth of ninepence!

Our next port of call was Thessalonica where we were allowed to disembark for a whole day. The sun was gloriously hot and we swam in the lovely warmth of the sea.

During the voyage a large contingent of battle - worn New Zealand soldiers joined us to make conditions even more cramped. They were fun, however - hilariously happy with their victories and filled with the prospect of beginning their journey home to their families. It was the beginning of 1945 and the hope of victory was very real. Our New Zealand colleagues, however, proved to be very boisterous and made life hazardous for us all, playing rugger with the furniture and generally creating a terrible noise on board. It was with great relief that we steamed into our final harbour. We were weary of continued lifeboat drills and alarms and for most of the two and a half weeks at sea the heat had been stifling. We longed to be on dry land and soon found ourselves docking at Port Said. We realised that we were destined for the Middle East!

Disembarkation was time-consuming and so noisy! All the local Egyptian Arabs were trying to sell us their different wares. To a certain extent we had been drilled and warned regarding the bargaining procedure but many of us were foolish. I myself bought a daily newspaper and only found afterwards that half of it had been sold to someone else!

A convoy of vehicles eventually transported us to Cairo and after having been assigned to a hotel were ordered to stay there until further instructions were given.

Almost every visitor to Cairo goes to Shepherd's

Hotel, and a boisterously large party of officers made this the target for our first night in the Middle East and a party to celebrate our arrival. We were all in uniform as civilian clothes were not permitted and we ate our meal outside in the relative cool of the evening. The meal served to us was delicious and a lot of drink was consumed. With much encouragement from members of the party I danced on the tables. We were thoroughly enjoying ourselves.

The following morning the telephone rang in our hotel and a message was passed to me telling me to report to Army Headquarters, Cairo. I reported and was shown into the presence of a senior ATS Officer. After saluting, I was told that I had been seen by many senior Army Officers dancing on the tables at Shepherd's Hotel. What a start to my overseas duty. I was severely reprimanded for my un-officer- like conduct and was extremely thankful to receive no further admonishment.

Before departing from this reprimand, I was told that I was to be posted to Palestine, to an Army Garrison, named Sarafand. 'You will proceed by train from Cairo in three days time,' came the order. 'That is all.' I left the office with reddened cheeks - blushing with embarrassment because of the rebuke and bursting with excitement to have received my posting.

3
Sarafand

The train from Cairo was packed full of troops and we crouched on every available bench. It was extremely hot and the unpadded seating made the train very uncomfortable. There were also innumerable Arabs who lay on the roof, waiting for their chance to relieve us of any of our items of valuables or luggage.

The train slowly meandered across the Sinai Desert and we travelled through Gaza to the more fertile and attractive land of Palestine. I sat smoking, gazing out of the train and idly pondering that I was entering the country where Jesus was born. Already many of the place names I was hearing were familiar from my Sunday School days.

The barren expanse of desert had given way to a green, mountainous place and the panorama before us was very beautiful yet somehow the heat seemed more intense here than in either the cities of the Mediterranean or the desert itself.

Before many hours passed we duly arrived at Sarafand. The Garrison itself covered miles of sandy ground and housed many thousands of troops and their families, all with their own headquarters, living quarters and offices. It was very comfortable and handsomely equipped with a hospital, school, a large transport centre and vast stables which housed hundreds of magnificent Arab horses. These stables I knew, provided the mounts for the cantonment's own hunt, 'The Ramle Vale'. I determined to join this as soon as possible.

All these I saw as the jeep bumped over the track to the bungalow in which I had been allocated a room. It was practically on the perimeter where a high wire fence stated the boundary of the cantonment. Just through the wire were vast orange groves and the exotic fragrance of the orange blossom welcomed me to my quarters. I was soon to find that their heady scent could at times become overbearing when any breeze blew it more strongly upon us.

The verandah of the bungalow was beautifully festooned with different coloured bougainvillea. Bright reds and purples shone up at me as I passed into the buildings and was taken to my room. It was neatly furnished and spotlessly clean and I noted with approval the white mosquito net folded on the bed. I was left to unpack and sat down briefly on the bed to survey my surroundings.

I suddenly noticed a long, unknown creature sitting on the mosquito net beside me. It appeared to be nodding at me. Was it about to pounce or was it dropping its head in a doze? I had seen plenty of bugs even in our short spell in Cairo but nothing as big or as menacing - looking as this. Jumping up, my only thought was to get rid of it and I rummaged about for something with which to kill it. I found a magazine and creeping up, I walloped it, killing it immediately. Suddenly ashamed of my ignorance and fear, I told nobody about it. It was a few days later that I saw another and was told that it was a Praying Mantis. They are quite harmless and fascinating to watch. They do not 'prey' but rather appear to 'pray', putting their long spindly 'arms' together and nodding their pin-like heads.

Sarafand is sixteen miles south of Jerusalem and five miles from both Tel-Aviv and Jaffa and it was a great deal hotter in this inland garrison than in any of these surrounding places. The heat made working or even walking quickly difficult as we became drenched in perspiration almost immediately. We soon adopted the Middle Eastern stroll, appearing very leisurely but conserving our energy as much as possible. We also came off duty at 1.00 pm having worked since 7.30 am and did not begin again until 5.30 in the evening to avoid the hottest part of the day. We did not waste time in prolonged siestas, however, but spent most afternoons playing tennis or travelling to Jaffa, near Tel-Aviv, to swim at the luxurious Club there.

We also had a well-equipped Officer's Club nearby and each Regiment occupied its own Mess. Ours was one of several which spread out like a fan around the edge of the cantonment. There we enjoyed excellent meals when those cooked for us by our Arab servants in the bungalow proved to be too regularly of giraffe which is very tough! They did keep our bungalow very clean, however, which we all appreciated and watched out for scorpions which had the nasty habit of creeping into any empty shoes. As an officer, I also had a bat-woman to care for me. She was a Cypriot and I became very attached to her.

One of the other privileges of the officer's life was that I was permitted to keep my own horse in the cantonment stables if I wished and to hire a 'syce', a servant, to care for him and this I did. Because of the extreme heat of the afternoons we would rise early in the mornings to exercise the horses or to take part in a hunt. Most mornings, therefore, at 6.00 am my syce would bring Chocolate, my Arab horse, to the bungalow. There he would sit and wait while I joined my friends, riding through the groves, picking ripe oranges, lemons or juicy grapefruit. We would watch the brilliantly coloured birds, the Rollers and Bee-Eaters which flitted proudly but silently through the trees. Unlike our blackbirds or starlings they have no song or cheeky whistle. When hunting we would venture further into the desert countryside chasing jackal. Instead of jumping hedges and fences we leapt over vicious - looking cacti with long, poisonous thorns. The incentive to keep one's seat was greatly increased!

I found my work in Sarafand very interesting. I was a junior Officer with two Palestinian ATS Officers and a British ATS Captain who was the Company Commander. We had two hundred Palestinian women to train, many of whom were very intelligent.

Some problems arose over language, however, as most Palestinians had Yiddish as their first language, although they also spoke English as well as Arabic. As a result they spoke whichever language suited them. To reduce this problem we took Arabic lessons ourselves, and this made domestic life simpler as well, as most of our civilian employees were Arabs.

During this comparatively peaceful time, I had opportunities for amazing and wonderful visits. Sometimes we would make the short journey to Bethlehem or Jerusalem where the St. David Hotel was regularly frequented for its delicious champagne and kippers!

The Biblically important sites became well known to us as we picnicked on the Mount of Olives and walked amongst the temples and holy areas of the city. I was interested in everything, not from a spiritual viewpoint but purely as a fascinated observer of humanity and I was equally intrigued by the religious solemnity of the Jews as by the regular devotion of the smiling Arabs. On one occasion we took jeeps and travelled south to the ancient site of Petra. The rose coloured stone of the carved buildings was beautiful and we surveyed them at our leisure as we took mules and meandered slowly through the city.

I loved this lifestyle with the camaraderie of the Mess and the companionship of so many who, like me, were determined to enjoy themselves to the best of their abilities. It was during this time that I became engaged to be married again. I had no real desire to be married but was lighthearted and enjoyed this romantic companionship. My succession of male friends was, however, by no means because of my attractiveness or personality but simply because there were so many British men and so few women - there was hardly any competition!

Drinking parties and daring visits to places which were even then out of bounds were our main evening activities. One of those visits took us to Beirut where the streets were notoriously dangerous although there was no bombing at that time. Four of us spent some leave there at the St. George's Hotel and visited some extremely seedy clubs in the city. The achievement of what was forbidden held a childlike fascination for us and we revelled in our brief escape from the garrison.

One night-time visit to Jaffa at this time sticks in my memory. When we arrived we would usually head for the night clubs which we knew but on this occasion we felt adventurous and scoured the city for one which we hoped would be more exciting. We arrived outside the black, shadowed door of a club behind which we could hear the dulled sounds of music and loud voices. Looking at each other mischievously, we strode to the door. I pushed it open.

The scene which met my eyes caused me to jolt to a halt and stand there gaping like a schoolgirl, for between the tables in the smoky light, the silvery flash of large knives flew viciously back and forth across the room! Before the others were barely through the door I issued an 'About Turn' and we stumbled back on to the street. That was just a little more exciting than we had bargained for!

Just prior to my first Christmas in Palestine I became bothered by pains in my abdomen. I was diagnosed as having a grumbling appendix and the medical officers suggested that I have an operation immediately.

'Now?' I cried in dismay. 'But it's almost Christmas and I'll miss all the fun!' I had cheerfully shed my fiancée by this time and was looking forward to the catalogue of parties planned in the Regiment. The Medical Officer reluctantly agreed to postpone the operation and I was allowed to enjoy the Christmas festivities.

Of my subsequent stay in hospital I remember very little apart from earning the censure of the Sister in charge because of two of my crazy friends. These two officers of a parachute battalion dashed in just as I was recovering from the anaesthetic and one of them pulled a bottle of gin out of his battle-dress top. 'Jill - wakey, wakey - Jill,' they called. 'A present for you.' They dashed off leaving me in my drousy state to quickly hide the bottle under the sheets!

In 1946, just after the war at home had ended, the terrorist activities in Palestine began with real ferocity. The Jewish/Arab hatred had boiled over and the roads became dangerous and were often mined. The Army ordered that all vehicles should travel in pairs for protection and never alone. Dreadful attacks were happening. Hostages were taken on many bombing raids and terrorists offensives. On one occasion a train carrying troops arriving from home was blown up and many soldiers were killed. No sooner had the news of this tragedy arrived than we heard that two British Sergeants had been murdered and their bodies strung up on gallows. The troops who found them went to cut them down but trod on a mine planted for them and they, too, were killed.

Soon it began to occur closer to home. In Sarafand terrorists stole a number of Parachute Regiment Uniforms and wore them driving into the Garrison. Inside the gates they opened fire upon troops who were being drilled on a parade ground nearby.

Next, a lorry filled with explosives was parked outside the office of the Officer - in - Command. The massive orchestrated explosion killed all those in the building and destroyed the building entirely. The danger of it all was becoming very real to us.

During this time I became deeply attracted to a crazy Irish Officer in the Trans -Jordan Frontier Force (TJFF). The TJFF were responsible for guarding the frontiers of Palestine and Jordan, and Sam was stationed at a place called Metulla, some distance from Amman, the capital of Jordan. Although travel was becoming increasingly difficult, I went to Metulla on many occasions when I was off duty. Sam, however, was discouraged from visiting me in Palestine as he had been accused by the Jewish terrorists of killing one of their people. He was warned to stay away as he had been black-listed and would be shot if he was ever spotted.

Sam was such fun and I always found his company

exciting. In him I found a kindred adventurous, if foolhardy, spirit and my friends became increasingly surprised at the duration of this relationship!

A dance in Metulla was a big attraction and when Sam asked me to accompany him, I determined that I would go. Unfortunately, I knew that permission for this trip would be refused because of the situation at Sarafand and the recent terrorist activities, so, undeterred, I decided to go without obtaining permission. I also wore the forbidden civilian clothes so I would not be spotted and set off by plane to Metulla.

We had a hilarious time. The party was well attended and Sam was always excellent company on these occasions. Attentive to me but also commanding attention from his friends, he would give full rein to his mad-cap, fun-loving personality.

I arrived back in Sarafand, full of the joviality of the weekend but also aware with some trepidation that my escapade could easily have been discovered. Sure enough, I was immediately called before no less personage than the Colonel. Waiting outside his office I began to admit to myself that this could be serious.

'Where were you at the weekend, Captain Gillette?' he barked, even before my hand had dropped from my salute. In what I thought was a suitably penitant voice, I told him. He informed me what he thought of my behaviour in a few, well-chosen cutting remarks and ended by saying, 'I would not have minded, Captain, if you had been killed. What I would have minded is if I had had to send my men out to get your body back. Dismissed!' Again, as in Cairo, I was extremely fortunate to receive no written report or official repercussions for my actions.

The terrorist activities continued with greater intensity during these months of 1946. In Jerusalem, the King David Hotel was bombed with the loss of ninety lives. Increasingly, the army came under attack, threatened by both sides: the Arabs considered us to be siding with the Jews, and the Jews hating us for working alongside the Arabs.

During this period I became the Company Commander of the women. One of my Palestinian Officers was an extremely clever and intelligent woman. Educated at Roedean, Leah had been a senior member of staff on the country's main newspaper, *The Palestinian Post*, before joining the British Army. We became friends and respected one another, on my part not least because she had command of no less than eight languages. My tentative attempts at Arabic seemed very poor in comparison.

Every weekend Leah requested permission to visit Jerusalem and this I granted. She never spoke of her activities at the weekend and initially I never thought of asking about them. Gradually, however, I became aware that after her departure the bombing and fighting seemed to intensify. Fearful of what I suspected, I asked her one day what she did at weekends and why she never stayed in the cantonment. She gave a non-committal answer. Allowing her to realise my suspicions, I mentioned that I considered that it would be easy to blow up my bungalow. Why did she think that had not happened? 'I happen to like you,' she replied, without a pause. In her situation, and more particularly, in mine, there was nothing I could do.

One day Sam phoned from Jordan to ask if I would go riding with him at the weekend and invited me to a party in the evening. I did not question his presence in the area knowing that to caution him would be futile and I arranged for him to call for me in the evening. I declined the ride as I knew I had various domestic chores to be done in the afternoon.

As I busied myself in my room I listened to the radio which buzzed away without me paying much attention. Suddenly, as I was getting ready for Sam's arrival, a news bulletin made me stop in my tracks. I stood frozen to the spot, hardly daring to breathe as I heard that two officers of the TJFF had been ambushed and shot whilst out riding locally. Both were dead.

I was still standing there dazed in the middle of the room when a knock came to my door. My friends had rushed round to find out if I had heard the news. So it was true. Sam and his friend had been killed.

Permission was given for me to attend the military funeral providing I was perfectly controlled. No emotion could be shown: discipline, not love, is the order in the Army.

Following this tragedy the Army gave me three months' leave to return to the United Kingdom. I was given the choice to remain in Britain if I wished or, alternatively to return to Palestine. Even before I had left and amidst the deep pain of this loss, I knew that my home was with my friends and with the Regiment in Palestine. I chose to return.

During these troubled times travelling was still made by sea. A long journey to the United Kingdom faced me and I was given ample opportunity for reflection. I think I was still deeply shocked by what had happened. I could not get out of my mind the fact that I was so nearly killed with Sam. If I had been with the riders I too would have been shot.

Something which would not go away lurked in the back of my mind and whispered the question, 'Why was my life spared?' I had no answer to give.

I spent my leave with my father whom I found had aged considerably and my two brothers who were settling back into civilian life. Dod had returned to his electrician's trade but Jack wanted to go on to bigger things. The disruption caused by the war began to make this possible for him and I was pleased to see his considerable talents put to use.

I did very little during this time and soon I was due to return to the Middle East. The journey was long and again my thoughts kept me company, my grief at losing Sam still being very hard to bear. It seemed that I was indeed returning a more sober and tame person!

4
Jerusalem

Instead of travelling by train from Cairo back to Palestine, I travelled by road with members of a Regiment who had also been on board the ship. Several vehicles travelled in convoy across the desert to Palestine. When we reached Gaza the convoy was challenged by the Jews. When they saw that I was travelling with them they thought for some reason that I was a spy. It became very tense. Eventually the Palestine Police appeared. Without much drama I was rescued by them and was put under their protection. I spent that night under lock and key in the Gaza Police Station!

The following day I was permitted to continue with the Regiment by road. All was peaceful until the very real scare of a mine across the road stopped the convoy. A wire had been spotted and traced to the side of the track. The Officer driving the vehicle in front asked me if I would prefer to walk or ride across the wires. I was terrified of riding across, but more ashamed of being thought a coward: the years of playing with my brothers had taught me never to allow that. I sat, therefore, beside this officer in the armoured car, perspiration running down my neck. We gingerly edged over the wires, feeling each wheel roll forward on - and on, until we crossed safely. All was well and we arrived back in Sarafand without further incident.

On my return I was informed that all soldiers' families were to be evacuated and all civilian employees dismissed. I was also informed that I had been given the unhappy task of organizing the former. It was an unenviable job. The wives of the officers and other ranks failed to understand why they should go and I should not. The fact that I was serving in the Army did not keep them from calling me unpleasant names and shouting rude remarks at me.

My main task in this distressing operation was to oversee the transportation of the evacuated families to Cairo and to report on their satisfactory accommodation there. After my return to Palestine from Britain I had been bitten by a dog and during the evacuation I had to undergo daily injections into my abdomen because of the threat of rabies. These were to last for fourteen days. On the thirteenth day I was ordered to fly to Cairo to supervise the settlement of the families. Because I had only one more rabies injection to receive I asked my Brigadier if I might be allowed to delay my visit to Cairo for one day until the injections were completed. Once more I came up against inflexible discipline of Army life: 'No. Take the serum with you and let the local hospital in Cairo give it to you,' was the reply. As a result I wasted hours waiting for treatment when I could have been more productively used completing the job I had been sent to do. Nevertheless, I had to obey orders without question as I had always been taught to do.

On my return to Sarafand from Cairo, I discovered that my work there was effectively finished, as the Palestinian ATS had been disbanded. The fighting between the Jews and Arabs had become so intense that it was considered safer for the majority of personnel to be moved from the area. More and more British soldiers were being ambushed and killed and I was soon moved to the British Army Headquarters in the King David Hotel in Jerusalem. It was late 1946 and I was to remain there for nearly two years.

I became a Staff Captain in Jerusalem under the General Officer Commanding troops in Palestine, General Sir Hugh MacMillan. He was an extremely efficient and highly esteemed officer. His great height (he was 6'3") and soldierly bearing reflected his personal stature as a well respected officer amongst his staff. I, of course, was mere 'small fry' as far as he was concerned.

The office in which I worked overlooked the Old City of Jerusalem and continually spasmodic firing rocketed around the building. It became quite normal for us to have to dive under our desks during the heaviest firing because so many of our windows were shattered. One of the officers from my section was shot in the knee during the shooting one day. I went with him to hospital and waited for him to emerge from the treatment room. The busyness of the hospital underlined for me how many casualties this war was producing. Queues of injured people were waiting to be seen and we could hear the guns and bombs which were causing it all very clearly as we sat in the hospital. While I was sitting there a young soldier walked alone into the waiting area. He had blood all over his face and I saw to my horror that he no longer had a nose. It had been shot away. He was walking carefully as though still dazed and he was clearly unaware of his injury and still in shock. The reality and pain were still to come.

Until this point I had been largely unaffected by the bombing. We had all had to accept it as part of life and carry on with our work. Having lived through the Blitz on London it was perhaps easier to accept. Having been confronted with this soldier, however, and all the suffering in the hospital that day, I was realising how devastating and painful the situation had become.

Soon after this I was driving into Jerusalem having been working in a village outside the city. With me was a very senior Palestinian Police Officer. Suddenly, from nowhere a young Jewish man sprang on to the road and stopped the car, pointing a revolver at us through the window. He ordered us out of the vehicle. 'Against the wall,' he yelled and pointed to one nearby with his gun. We fully expected to be shot in an instant, or at the very least to be held hostage. I was sure I was about to die and a rigid terror filled me. Never before had I been so unspeakably frightened. My ears strained to hear the 'click' of his gun as he prepared to shoot.

I do not know why or how but some minutes later we were ordered back into our car and commanded to proceed. We were being let go! I shook so much I could barely drive and my body was still quivering when we reached the city and I remained shocked for a long time afterwards. Again I had escaped what had appeared to be, and which for so many others in identical circumstances had been, certain death. I was too shaken to even consider why it had happened. I only knew that I had been completely terrified, to say nothing of the jittering V.I.P. in the passenger seat! Thereafter I was never allowed out without an escort of four armed men.

It had become apparent that it was entirely unsafe for the British to maintain their occupation and some alternative would have to be sought. Ships of immigrant Jews were trying to land and they flooded into the country from other lands, and especially from Europe where so many atrocities had been enacted upon them. The British were instructed to prevent the ships from docking and immigrants from landing as it was impossible to accommodate the continual arrivals. It became progressively distressing and some solution had to be sought. History tells us how the Government concluded that the only answer to this very sad state of affairs was to hand over the Mandate and to declare Palestine the state of Israel.

As soon as this was announced the British prepared for their inevitable withdrawal from the country. For some time I had been one of only two ATS officers in Palestine, therefore one of only two women and this remained so during the closing months of the British Army's occupation. My brother, Jack later wrote to me from London saying that he had not heard from me for so long but was very pleased to read in *The Daily Telegraph* that I had been one of the two ATS officers last out of Palestine.

Shortly before our final departure in May, 1948 I was invited to a dinner party. It is one of the peculiarities of the British Army that even in the midst of this bloody and vicious war there were still cocktail and dinner parties to attend. At this particular dinner I was seated opposite a tall and distinguished officer of the Argyle and Sutherland Highlanders.

If someone had asked me prior to that evening if I believed in love at first sight or even at first meeting, I would have scorned the question. But I can only say that this is what happened that evening when I sat with this man. It was as if no one else was there. He was so different from everybody else with whom I had worked or travelled, different from all the chaps with whom I had been to parties or had even been engaged to. This was a gentleman, polite in his speech and gentle in his manner and highly decorated for his war-time service. His name was Rex Beatty. Suddenly and inescapably I fell in love with Rex and he with me!

The final month of occupation was extremely busy but Rex and I stole what little time we could to be together. It was not conducive to a blossoming romance and, in addition, I soon discovered that Rex, for all his success in the Army and the respect he commanded from his fellow officers, was not happy. I was always aware that there was something which greatly troubled him but about which he found it very hard to talk. He soon told me, however, what it was. Rex was married, unhappily and they had a baby girl. They had not been married for long but an uneasy estrangement existed between him and his wife. We both knew that the situation was extremely difficult. Having left Jerusalem we met up briefly in Egypt but our meetings, for all that I loved to be near him, were always tinged with the shadow, not only of impending separation, but also at the deep sadness that our love could never be as happy or as enjoyed as it might have been.

The final day in May 1948 arrived. It was the day of our departure and we prepared for a last look at this beautiful land so torn yet still to face so much fighting and turmoil. There seemed little to leave behind. Even my flat in the nearby barracks had been looted. The Arab servants had nothing to lose by helping themselves: nobody in the British Army would be left to charge them. As we prepared to depart they sat there grinning at us with those smiles I had often mistrusted and behind which other more malignant emotions seemed to hide.

Our convoy left. All the senior officers were driven in bullet - proof cars, junior officers like myself travelled in what the Army call 'half - tracks' which are only half protected vehicles and left us very vulnerable should there be an attack. We drove slowly and carefully in a long, closely guarded convoy of vehicles, hearing the firing threateningly close to us as we drove to the airport. It was so dangerous that it was necessary for us to crouch low to get safely from the cars on to the aircraft. Dashing across the tarmac to the safety of the plane we came under machine gun fire and we were more than grateful to leave Jerusalem for Haifa to await our later evacuation to Egypt.

During the four years I spent in this wonderful land my eyes were opened to our magnificent surroundings: the vivid colours; the brilliance of the flowers, like the anemones which carpeted the shores of the Sea of Galilee in springtime; the magnificence of the expanse of dry land going to and away from the Dead Sea; the amazing ancient carvings on the deserted buildings at Petra, so old and cave-like, and the port of Aqaba which in those years had nothing at all except the Arab huts.

They were also opened to the bitter hatred which had initiated and fanned this awful war, both sides so opposed to one another and to us: the intelligent, hard - working Jews hating us and cleverly fighting us; the Arabs, easy and always smiling and pleasant whatever bitterness was beneath this calm mask.

My spiritual eyes, however, remained firmly closed to the significance attached to the places which I visited and in which I worked: Bethlehem, Nazareth and Jerusalem.

I have no desire to return there. My memories are very precious and I understand that the country is now very different but the fighting still continues.

May, 1948, brought my final farewell to Palestine, no longer known by that name, but changed as the Jews crowded into their homeland, to Israel.

5
All Change

The carriage chugged effortlessly along the track, and seated facing the engine, I stared out of the window at the rain-soaked countryside. Huge, elongated rain drops streaked the glass but were quickly swept away by the speed of the train. The autumn colours of the trees and heather refused to be dimmed by the dull skies and obscuring rain and I thoroughly enjoyed the changes in the landscape and climate which I had unconsciously missed.

It was September, 1949 and I had finally returned to Britain from the Middle East earlier that year. I had stayed on overseas duty for as long as the Army allows, completing my final year in Ismalia, in Egypt. After service in Palestine we had found Egypt refreshingly safe and its history interesting, but distinctly lacking in the beauty and variety which we had previously enjoyed. Rather shamefully, we found the wonders of Egypt decidedly dull!

I also missed Rex. The Argyle and Sutherland Highlanders had returned to the United Kingdom but, always wanting to be in the thick of all the action, Rex had volunteered to go to Malaya for a duty of three years and fight the bandits in the jungle there. Many of the ex-Palestine Police Force had also been seconded to Malaya at this time.

Rex had told me that he was the son of ex-missionaries in China. He and two of his sisters had, in fact, been born in China where his father had been a surgeon. He had been brought up in a Christian household and had himself started theological training having received his schooling at Trent College, Nottinghamshire. Something, however, had made Rex change and rebel against all this. It may have been a gradual decline in interest and commitment, hardly perceptible to an onlooker, but when war broke out Rex ran away to join the Army. He fought in many battles, many theatres of war and was awarded the Military Cross for magnificent courage during the Eighth Army's advance against Rommel's Forces.

Although we had known each other for so short a time, Rex and I both felt that we were somehow linked. After he had gone, there always seemed to be something missing; nothing I could put my finger on but some emptiness in all I did and wherever I went. Being a naturally buoyant and self-sufficient person, I found these feelings very strange. The bond between us had only grown as we had written regularly but the shadows remained both because of the distance between us and because of the circumstances which would remain even if he was nearby.

One cause for celebration occurred in Ismalia, however. One morning on duty I was notified that I had received a commendation. I became overwhelmed both with emotion and embarrassment. A large lump rose in my throat as I was presented with the award of 'Mentioned in Despatches' for distinguished service. This is an engraved bar in the shape of an oakleaf which is fixed on the ribbon of the Palestine medal. I did not deserve this as I had served with others whose devotion to duty was far greater than mine (I was only too aware of my own lack of discipline!) and there were yet others who had been in the forefront of battle but who had received no decoration. I felt very unworthy but very honoured.

Now here I was back in Britain. My new job involved a lot of travelling about the north - east of England and the whole of Scotland as the Staff Officer Physical Training (SOPT). I travelled long distances in this new post visiting the various camps and training centres but I enjoyed the freedom and flexibility that this involved. I found myself returning to Edinburgh's Redford Barracks where I had myself trained as an Officer Cadet. I chuckled to myself when I remembered how mature and refined I thought I had become in this female camp in Edinburgh. I also greatly treasured touring Scotland, about which I had previously known little and was thrilled by the magnificent beauty I saw in the

Highlands as I travelled to Fort George and further afield.

By now I was in my early thirties and was considering what my next stage in my life would be. The Army had been very good to me and I also knew that I enjoyed Army life. Indeed, I loved it. The Army at home and in peace time was very different from an Army at war but I decided to remain and applied for a regular commission. This involved attending a five-day course in Wales where physical and mental tests were carried out as we underwent constant intensive training. We were expected to have our skills examined, first with awful 'intelligence' tests - fitting all sorts of pieces of wood together and puzzling over strange sequential numbers - and then outdoors, subjected to assault courses, swinging precariously on ropes over rivers and crawling purposelessly through overgrown woodland.

Having survived the London Blitz, journeyed through mined seas and roads and spent four years in Palestine in the midst of civil war and terrorist attacks, I was haughtily unamused by tests I considered to be futile and irrelevant. Some I did not even try! Finally, the five days ended by being interviewed by a General and other high-ranking officers. To my utter amazement, I passed. I received my commission in the regular Army.

It was soon after I took up the post of Commandant of the Women's Army Training School at Aldershot that Rex wrote me with extraordinary news and with his proposal: his wife had died two years previously of the crippling disease, poliomyelitis and he was returning to the United Kingdom - and would I marry him?

The news was so unexpected that I was unsure of what to think. Over two years had passed since we had seen each other and questions jumbled about in my head. How could I be sure that I would really feel the same way about him as I had? Did I really want to leave the Army which I loved? In those days females had to leave the Army when they married and I felt I had no home to which I could go. It was still with a perplexed and undecided mind that I travelled to Southhampton in early September, 1951 to meet Rex's ship as he arrived from Malaya. Even as I stood on the quay, my heart pumping excitedly, I did not claim to know my own mind. As soon as I saw him waving to me, however, as soon as I saw him rushing towards me, as soon as I was near him and had been in his company a few short hours, I knew that not only did I love him more than ever but I also knew that without hesitation I would marry him.

The wedding arrangements were soon under way. Rex had been posted to Fort George as the Officer-in-charge of Training, rather a long way from Aldershot, but nearer than Malaya! We planned to have a short engagement, the marriage to take place in January, 1952. It was to be a military wedding with the service held in a small church in Aldershot and the reception given to me by the officers of the Army School of Physical Training in the Officers' Mess.

There were some complications as there are in all weddings. I had no real home of my own from which to leave and my father who was suffering badly from Parkinson's Disease was nervous regarding giving me away. In addition, clothes were still rationed and nobody held sufficient clothing coupons to purchase a wedding outfit, least of all me. Rex and his best man were resplendent in full Highland dress uniform, of course, and somehow I managed to borrow a wedding dress and the rest of the regalia for the exciting day. It was all provided so happily and willingly that this was enough to make it perfect.

My future 'in-laws' did not come to our wedding. This greatly puzzled me but I was not unduly perturbed. I was marrying Rex because I loved him, and he loved me. I thought I was considered 'not bad'! Quite a lot of the undesirable nastiness had disappeared, but perhaps I was not as acceptable as they would have desired for their only son. One of his sisters did look in at our reception where we were partaking of champagne very moderately. She did not stay long.

After a short honeymoon in London, Rex took me to his home in Nottinghamshire, a pretty village where his father was the Doctor. Here I was to live until Rex could find married quarters.

Following the initial introductions on arrival, Rex and I tried our best to disappear on some pretext. I had a small Scottie dog but Rex's parents did not like animals in the house and we had determined to get him in somehow. We were like nervous children trying to smuggle this dog of mine up the back stairs! How I would keep him I had no idea.

I was really rather terrified of my father-in -law and mother-in-law, both so correct, kind and austere, and after so much freedom for many years I was petrified at the thought of being left in his home when Rex had to return on duty at Fort George.

These fine folk were so good and caring for so many. My father-in-law had his own dispensary attached to their house and my mother-in-law helped him. He was also a lay-reader in the Church of England and had years of experience as a missionary in China - oh, dear, I was so different, so out of place, and I was left alone with them with a hidden dog!

I was in my early thirties but for the days I was there I felt like a little girl wondering how to behave. I dared not tell them about my years in the Army so I started by trying to be helpful. Like the guest I was, I made my bed and tidied my room. When I told my mother-in-law she briskly asked me to undo the bed again as somebody from the village came in to help!

Sunday arrived and I was even more frightened. I did not mind going to church - I had, at least, my childhood knowledge to draw upon - but I was told that in the evening people gathered together in the drawing room and sang hymns round the piano. Such intrusion of the religious into the homely and familiar unsettled me. In addition, I had little knowledge of hymns and when I was invited to choose one I showed my ignorance in knowing only one which I could choose. I was probably not supposed to notice the concerned and mildly humoured faces of the visitors which remained too firmly fixed on their hymn books. I could not really fathom the family's disapproval, however, although my many differences from them were plain to see.

To my great joy a married quarter was quickly given to Rex just outside Nairn in Moray. I felt that on my own with Rex I could be myself, free from the embarrassment I had felt with the kindly hostility I had felt from his parents. This was also to be our very first home and I loved it. The house itself was rather plain but it had glorious views of the surrounding hills and was only walking distance from the beautiful golf course which I could cross and gaze upon the Moray Firth looking over towards the Black Isle.

After three extremely happy months together, the longest time we had ever been in the same city since our meeting, we journeyed to England to bring Diana, Rex's daughter, then three years old, back to be with us. She was a lovely little girl with curling gold hair and a sunny smile and we were very happy together as she quickly settled in. It was lovely to be a part of the family which we had become as, in particular, she got to know her Daddy who had been away for so long. This family was also due to expand. I was truly overcome with joy when I discovered, almost immediately after Diana came to us, that a baby was on the way.

I was not very surprised when Rex expressed a wish for us to start attending a church in Nairn. He had started to regularly read his Bible at home and when I had asked him why he read it he gently and simply told me that it was a wonderful book. He said that when he had been fighting with the Eighth Army his father had sent him a letter containing the text, 'Seek ye first the kingdom of God,' and he had always remembered it. It seemed that this had marked a rekindling of his interest in spiritual things which he had abandoned when he left college to join the army. But if Rex wanted to go to church, I was very happy to go with him. I wanted to be a part of everything he wanted, I loved him so much. When I tried reading the Bible, however, I found it all very dull. I would open it up when I was alone, trying to understand how or why reading it every day should mean so much to Rex. It was becoming increasingly important to him but I was baffled by it all.

The church in Nairn was vastly different from my early memories of church going. Here we sat to pray: I thought everyone knelt! There were very long prayers and the congregation sat silently, making no response. I even turned a few heads when I repeated an 'Amen'. They did not even speak to each other either going in or coming out and they all looked extremely unhappy. It somehow felt unseemly that I should feel so happy in contrast. In addition, I was sadly ignorant. I could not find my way around the pages of the Bible which were as thin and inseparable as roll-your-own cigarette papers, and I 'crinkled' noisily after others had begun to follow the reading. I did not know any of the Psalms which they sang and very few hymns. Although I had spent ten years in the Army I cannot remember ever attending a church service during this time, even for church parades, which were not demanded of officers. In particular, to hear people speaking of Jesus was unusual. I couldn't remember anybody ever speaking to me of him since my Sunday School days.

Just before Christmas a beautiful baby daughter was born to us in the Nairn Cottage Hospital, now the Nairn Town and County Hospital. We were thrilled with this perfect baby and Diana gazed with awe and love at her tiny sister. We named her Dawn and soon we were home together.

During this time Rex had become increasingly keen to serve Overseas again in the Army. He had waited until the baby was born but soon afterwards volunteered for service. He had found the Army in active service much more appealing than the Training Post he had been involved in at home so we prepared our little family for life abroad.

As it turned out Rex left for his post in Nigeria a month after Dawn was born and it was another five months before married quarters became available for us at Enugu where Rex was based.

My memories of our two years in Nigeria are limited. I remember fondly the beautiful and brilliantly coloured plants and trees - the frangipani and the flame of the forest - and the heady fragrances they gave. I also remember the Eboe

Nigerians, the blackest of black Africans, joyfully playing with the children in our compound. The Africans love children and Isaac, one of our 'boys' held his arms out to take Dawn from me even as we arrived at our new home. Dawn was delighted and I will always be able to recall the joy on Isaac's face as this golden-haired baby so readily went to him.

Perhaps my memories are sketchy because little happened. Like most mothers my priority was my children and the landmarks in my life were their achievements and progress. There were many snakes and flying ants we caught by placing bowls of water under lights. The servants would pull off the ants wings and then eat them. Most of the other Officers' wives had daily 'canasta' parties - a card game which was harmless but which wasted many hours. I was not interested - but not because I considered it a shade inferior to bridge! No, I was aware that I was changing within myself. While we were in Nigeria there was time to think and to discuss and we also attended a tiny Anglican church just outside the town. Rex had never reprimanded or lectured me into changing in the way in which he had. Instead, he had prayed and prayed. Amy Carmichael writes in her book, *Edges Of His Ways* that, 'Sometimes there is a great deal to be done before God can come upon us in changing and renewing power.' Certainly the change was under way and what was to be a gradual process for me had begun.

Rex also spoke a great deal about how many

important prophecies in the Bible had been fulfilled even during the time we had been in Palestine. He showed me Jeremiah 32: 8-15 which foretells the buying and selling of land and the procedure this would involve. Rex said that his Regiment had been responsible for the buying and selling of land and that the prophecy was fulfilled as the Jews and Arabs had gathered together for these transactions. My own knowledge of prophecy had been non-existent but I became deeply interested and remain so.

As time passed Rex came to the momentous decision to resign his regular commission from the Argyle and Sutherland Highlanders and move into civilian life. He had never felt that he was suited to the Army in peace - time which was so different from the war and the battle zones where he had served. But as we flew home to the United Kingdom to this new life I was nervous: Rex had no job; we had no home; we had no particular plans. We only had the meagre wealth of £2,000 which Rex had been given as a gratuity for his fifteen years of Army Service.

With the help of a mortgage we bought a bungalow with a large garden on the outskirts of Newcastle-upon Tyne. Rex also bought a cheap, second-hand car, and eagerly went forth to find employment. He soon discovered, however, that this was far from simple. There were numerous decorated officers and men from all the Services searching for work.

Determined and anxious to provide for us, and also learning that another baby was on the way, Rex began by trying door-to-door selling of encyclopaedias! He found this very hard but did not complain. The salary was non-existent - just commission on the books sold. I economized by making all our bread, cakes and biscuits, and fruit juices, and Rex planted vegetables and fruit bushes in the garden. He changed his job and began another trying to sell typewriters. This time he visited firms and shops. Again commission on sales was the only reward.

It would not be true to state that our situation was smooth and easy. There were days when I had not got enough money to pay the paper bill and I would hurry past the shops until I could pay. But we were undeniably happy, both with each other and in our growing family. At times, however, my heart was heavy and it ached for him. The whole of his background had been so different, so guided and protected: boarding school; public school; Bible College; Missionary Society College with Harry Sutton and many other well - known Evangelical men; and then fifteen years in the Army. He was unsuited to the salesmanship and solitariness of this new life to which he had been forced to adapt.

Rex still read his Bible, and daily readings and prayers were taken with the children at breakfast time. He also returned to his Biblical studies in his spare time and it was not long before he became a lay-reader in the Church of England and was greatly used to preach in the villages and towns on the outskirts of Newcastle. Northumberland is a beautiful county and I loved going with him to many famous old churches.

Arriving quite early one summer Sunday evening at a small village church the cows followed us to the gate. An elderly man welcomed us and Rex asked if anybody would ring the bell. The old man nodded to me and said, 'You'll do!' I gamely grabbed the rope and swung on it hard but all my efforts produced the most ridiculous 'ting'. This small church had arches everywhere and the preacher sat behind one of them. As I sat in the hard pews I felt like a child again, trying to suppress my giggles as Rex leaned forward precariously from the pulpit to announce the hymns and peered round the arches, this way and that, to conduct the service.

During those months I was listening and learning and also mixing with other Christians. I was slowly becoming acquainted with evangelical language and the 'do's' and 'don't's' of Christian life. I still smoked and enjoyed a drink before an evening meal, however, and when we were invited out to friends' homes for dinner, I unconsciously waited for the drinks to be served. They never were and I so much wanted a cigarette, but the idea was out of the question. When Christians came to us for an evening meal I would hide my cigarettes and try to wave the offending smell out of the window. Although my lifestyle had begun to be affected I was still baffled by such questions as, 'Are you saved?' I did not know what I was supposed to say.

We began worshipping in a Free Independent

Evangelical Church where most of the members had come from a Brethren Assembly. I encountered lots of helpful teaching but also more unspoken rules. On one occasion I was invited to speak to the ladies about my experiences in Palestine. Perhaps I did not tell them what they had expected to hear but I also went without wearing a hat and I sat on the table to speak. Perhaps my lipstick was also noticeable! I was unaware not only that I was upsetting all ladies present, but that I was also offending them and making terrible and previously unknown *faux pas*. Nobody at the meeting said a word but later I met friends who stopped me saying, 'I heard this,' or 'I heard that.' I think they were partly shocked themselves but were partly enjoying the raising of eyebrows I seemed to cause.

It was while we were attending this church that I was invited to go to a friend's house to a meeting. An ex-dance band leader was to speak and tell us of his conversion to Jesus Christ. For all that I had been changing slowly myself I knew that this 'conversion' was what I had never known or understood. I sat at the back of a large room packed to capacity with people. This man gripped my attention as I listened to him telling us of how his life of swearing, drinking and gambling had been changed by Christ.

I identified so much of my life with this, and although my swearing and smutty stories had gone, I knew that it was because I loved Rex and our children so much that I was partially changed. I was still self-centred within myself. Tears were trickling down my face. The same man was speaking again elsewhere. I wanted to hear more, indeed I could hardly wait until I heard him again. It was at this second meeting that I decided to ask Jesus to take my past away, to forgive me and to give me the life which had Jesus at the centre of it instead of my own wishes. I wanted this Jesus to be real to me.

At home I knelt by my bed confessing all the wasted years and asked Jesus to take my life and use it for himself. I had been given so much I did not deserve but now I was beginning to understand. This was the change which Amy Carmichael had written about, the power with which God comes, and towards which I had been gradually moving, for all these years.

Rex was smiling. His prayers had been answered as I shared in what had been his for a long time. In my eagerness I asked him what perhaps seemed an unusual question: 'Do you love Jesus more than me?' I was more than a little taken aback when he answered, 'Yes, indeed I do.' Clearly this changing proccss was not over - I had so much still to learn.

6
Family Matters

On 9th December 1954, our son was born. I had not been well during my pregnancy and had spent the latter months in hospital. Even with all the bed and rest and monitoring, the baby was born very prematurely. He weighed only 4lbs. and was a tiny bundle of a child, very yellow and very wrinkled. At first glance we knew that he was unwell and we were given him to hold as he was not expected to live. The pessimism was underlined when we were asked if we would like to nave him baptised immediately. We did, and named him David Rex. As we cradled this tiny baby in our arms, Rex and I cried together. We were filled with grief at the obvious lack of hope given to us and at the sickly appearance of the child. Soon he was taken from us and put into an incubator and we were left alone, comforting each other in the quietness which was between us.

About eight hours after this, however, a doctor came to tell us that contrary to all predictions, our son's breathing was getting stronger and stronger - so strong that he was crying gustily! This tiny baby who was not expected to live had been spared and we gladly gave thanks to God for his goodness. As the days passed, David continued to cry and wail. I was told that this is quite frequently the way in which premature babies fight back. Whether or not this is true, it helped us to look on the bright side as our baby exercised his lungs!

David grew into a sturdy little fellow. He grew accustomed to seeing men speaking from a pulpit, including his father and at a very early age he would attempt to imitate them. He would arrange the various stools in the house to make steps, put a white towel or something similar round his neck and copy the Church of England vicars with their vestments and their white 'stoles'. He enticed his sisters and anybody else he was able to coerce to sit around and listen to his 'preaching'.

Dawn similarly had those whom she wished to copy. She informed us at an early age that she would like to be a 'church lady'. This, we discovered was a member of the choir and she thought this a worthy ambition from her reasoning that 'everybody would stand up when I go into church' as they do in the Church of England when the clergy and choir enter.

Our early family days were very happy. Rex and I seemed to be growing closer and closer as God's Holy Spirit was now able to work in us jointly. We entered into the life of our church wherever we could and we became interested in the Overseas Missionary Fellowship (O.M.F.). Rex changed his job and began working for a firm of Insurance Brokers. Although his heart was not really in insurance, he did very well. He began to travel more with his work and he enjoyed the contact with many people in business, boldly using opportunities to speak about his Lord. Whenever possible he would bring the conversation round to politics and current affairs. So many would comment on the events taking place and being a student of prophecy, Rex would frequently take out his small pocket Bible and quote what God's Word said on the matter.

Our life-style had become very different from our Army days. The Army is really a world of its own. Everything is provided for but now we had to fend for ourselves and even this took some getting used to. Certainly it was a struggle at times but we were repeatedly shown that 'the Lord sometimes gives more, but always all we need'. In particular, we were provided for when holidays came as an acquaintance offered us their holiday bungalow in Southerness, near Dumfries for nine years running. Thus we regularly enjoyed two wonderful weeks in a cottage right on the sea-front which was a perfectly safe place for the children.

We also attended Family Houseparties in Wales, run by the Officers' Christian Union. They were tremendous fun as we spent most of our days playing games, swimming in the outdoor pool or going to the beach. In the morning and again after the evening meal, the children and young folk had their own groups for Bible Study, prayer and discussion and the adults had theirs also.

I always felt that I learned so much from mature, loving Christian men and women at these house-parties. So many people - missionaries, church leaders, other parents, youngsters in the forces - filled with a love for God and sharing their exciting experiences. I felt so lacking in knowledge and maturity about Christian things but I did feel that I was learning.

One of the most obvious changes in me was my smoking. For years I had continued smoking, pretending to cut down and hiding the cigarettes. I was so stupidly hooked. Even my children with their usual candour told me that Christians should not smoke! Eventually I had to give up pretending and trying and I pleaded with God to take this dirty, addictive habit away and to make me feel clean. He did just that - overnight! I did, in my weakness still keep a few cigarettes hidden for a year or two, but I have never smoked again.

When the children became a little older I answered an advertisement in the local paper which read, 'Physical Training teacher required, part-time to teach at the Jewish Theological Seminary for Girls in Gateshead'. The job seemed purpose - made for me but there were no other Gentiles employed in the seminary and it seemed unlikely that I would get the job. It was with great surprise, therefore that I received the news that I had been appointed.

My task was really to teach these Jewish girls who

came from all over the world how to teach Physical Education to others. Many of them were very intelligent although initially the language barrier prevented them from joining my class, and they started with me in their second year. Some, however, were expert linguists already speaking up to nine languages. They were all strict orthodox Jewesses and many of them planned to go to Israel after they graduated. Having lived for over four years in Palestine, I was able to picture many of the places they talked about and we all enjoyed the classes more because of this. They were delightful people and teaching them was more of a privilege than a mere job.

I did have one student, however, who was not an easy pupil. Because of this she stood out more noticeably from the others who were so diligent and bright. On making enquiries I was told that she had been born in Ravensbruk Concentration Camp. Her entire family had been murdered in the gas chambers. I could see how the shadow of war, which everyone tried to forget with varying success, darkened everything for this pupil of mine. Her whole life, even from her birth was scarred by it. So much could be ignored or erased from memory but the horror of this war was ingrained in her like the Ravensbruk number tattooed on her arm. I eventually lost touch with her and her colleagues but I think of them often, living and working in their new Israel; intelligent, hard-working but bound up in a legacy of hatred out of which they try to salvage something positive for themselves.

After I began this job we were able to move to a larger home. Apart from being more comfortable, some of the rooms were more spacious and this allowed us to hold house-meetings, inviting speakers to come and address those who came. We discovered that sending out about a hundred invitations would usually attract between thirty and forty people, many of them non-Christians, and they were happy days as several people were converted. One evening a number of young students from Newcastle University came to hear a pharmacist who was a Christian speak. Three of them decided to follow Jesus and are still going strong for the Lord.

It was a great thrill for us when, at the age of fifteen, Dawn gave her heart to Jesus. She was a lively, active senior schoolgirl - always happy and regularly inviting her school friends to come to our church. Four of her friends were baptised there. A year later Dawn sat and passed nine "O" Levels and her Headmistress was keen for her to continue her schooling and apply for University when the time came. But Dawn had other plans, changed from the days when as a little girl she had wanted to be a 'church lady'. Her longing now was not to join the choir but to be a 'church lady' in another sense: she had set her heart firmly on becoming a Missionary Nurse. So determined was she that she persuaded the Matron of our local hospital to accept her as a cadet nurse and she left school and started work at a teaching hospital at the age of seventeen.

Our interest in the Overseas Missionary Fellowship

has always remained, perhaps due to our years living abroad, and once a month an OMF prayer meeting was held in our home. During his business travels Rex, always persuasive and positive, encouraged others to open their homes also for prayer and this they did in Sunderland, in Jesmond, in Newcastle and in Morpeth and other surrounding areas. It is always exciting to see growth and we were delighted as God was positively answering our prayers. One sign of this was that David too had given his young heart to Jesus.

It was still with much trepidation, however, that we agreed to arrange a valedictory (or farewell) service for twelve new OMF missionaries, having been asked to book Newcastle's City Hall which held 2000 for the occasion. Our minds boggled at the size of the hall and we tried not to be too sceptical about the possibility of filling it. We would have to pray hard while we made the arrangements and leave the rest to God.

Alan Redpath was to be the speaker that night and when the evening arrived we took the missionaries out for a meal before going on to the City Hall. As we arrived we saw people streaming into the building and were beside ourselves with joy as it was soon filled to capacity. This was a wonderful if simple lesson to us of how God answers our prayers even when we pray with the merest scrap of faith. It was something we were to remember and cling on to in the following months, gradually marvelling at how surprised we were when God answered our prayers. He always answered: sometimes it would be *yes*, sometimes *no,* sometimes *wait*.

7
Dawn

It was the evening of 23 February, 1970 and Rex, Dawn and I went to the prayer meeting held in our church. Dawn was usually a keen participant so I was surprised when I noticed her slipping from the room with one of her friends during a session of prayer. As they did not return I became worried and I crept out myself. I found Dawn outside being very violently and unnaturally sick. Her eyes also looked strange and she was holding her head, saying it felt as if it were about to burst. Something was clearly terribly wrong. I rushed inside and signalled to Rex to come. In the few minutes it took him to leave the room Dawn was becoming worse and worse and we immediately drove our daughter at high speed to our excellent General Practitioner. On the way the police even stopped us for speeding but when they saw the urgency they assisted us at even greater speed.

As she was virtually carried into the hospital, Dawn was holding her head and moaning, clearly in great distress and she was whisked away from us as soon as we arrived. We had to merely sit and wait, hour after hour. Eventually we were advised to go home and wait there. We cried many tears that night and thereafter. We had read of crying to the Lord and wetting the floor with our tears: this we did. I felt so terribly frightened and helpless and although we prayed I knew in my heart that I was leaning more heavily on Rex than on the Lord - and what could Rex do?

On our return to the hospital the next morning we were told that Dawn had suffered a brain haemorrhage. A neuro-surgeon told us that the damage was to the front of the brain and the prospect of recovery or even survival looked fairly bleak - an operation stood little hope of success.

Days passed as Dawn lay in hospital closely monitored for any improvement. Our lovely, active daughter was unresponsive and lying silently in the white bed of her room. It seemed that normal life had been suspended for us all. David was at home with us studying for his O' levels at school. He loved his sister deeply and was greatly affected by the traumas of her sudden illness. Such was the depth of this teenage experience he wrote a most moving essay during English language at school, recording his insights and feelings during these long months. Diana had left home but was living nearby so she was able to come and visit Dawn.

Sometimes I wondered how it was possible to shed so many tears but still to keep on crying. Our friends gathered round to support us and the prayers which were requested were willingly offered up by so many of them. The elders gathered round her bed and we all knelt in prayer but I found it so hard to pray for God's will when in my heart I so desperately wanted her to live.

Some days later the surgeon rang to ask Rex to come to see him at the hospital where they would discuss a brain operation to which Rex would have to give his consent. Friends gathered with us to ask the Lord to give Rex the right decision and they stayed with me pleading with God to guide my beloved husband in this difficult decision. When he arrived he was greeted with the news that Dawn had suffered an aneurism (further bleeding) and was in a coma. This was the Lord's answer as an operation was now impossible. It was so difficult to accept or understand.

Dawn remained in the coma for some days. During that time we did not know what affect the haemorrhage and the subsequent bleeding may have had upon her and we were not cheered by the discouraging information which the doctors gave to us. We could only wait and watch. She looked so beautiful and peaceful. We wondered what could be happening to our daughter inside and beneath this passive exterior.

Miraculously, the Lord did bring Dawn out of the coma. The doctors had considered that this was unlikely to happen so we rejoiced that this step had been taken. But Dawn was lost and confused. It seemed that her brain was in great disorder and as soon as she could move she began throwing anything given to her around the room. She even tore at the clothes put on her and the hospital staff had to resort to tying her wrists to the sides of her bed. How our hearts ached to see our daughter bound like this and to see the frenzy and distress which had necessitated it. She was also unable to communicate with us or even speak. This dreadful disorder of Dawn's mind lasted for some months, during which her lovely face was quite expressionless, whereas before it had shone with enthusiasm, health and energy. Dawn herself heard the sister of the ward say that she would be a vegetable and indeed during this period it appeared that this dreadful term did describe her mental state. We were also told that she had lost the use of her right leg and that her balance was severely affected.

During these difficult months I was allowed to spend all day at the hospital where I would sit with her and as she gradually became calmer I encouraged her to try simple tasks. I would help her say words and sentences or with a pencil and paper she would try to write, the writing all shaky and crooked down one side of the page. I had been told, however, that there have been patients who have come out of comas with their brains functioning enough for them to re-learn some of what had been lost. We prayed that this would be the case and we were strengthened to carry on by the prayers of others.

I knew that I must, must, must lean more upon God and I began to find myself slowly and fearfully doing just that. I prayed that I might love Jesus at least as much as I loved my husband and children. During conversations with Rex he was explaining that Jesus must always come first. It was something which had always disturbed me and had been one of my first questions after my conversion. But I found it so hard. We knew in our heads that we should but I found it so difficult in practise. It was a long, testing time.

Before going into Dawn's ward each day I would go into the hospital chapel to plead with God and to try to control my own nervousness. It was so heart-breaking to enter her ward sometimes. She was doubly incontinent and there were times when the filthy, ugly sight greeting us as we entered would make us tremble for her future.

We gradually received encouragement, however. It appeared that the damage Dawn had incurred was to the part of her brain which controlled her emotions rather that her intellect. This was causing the impassive face and lack of expression or reaction. One day, however, I took a mirror into the ward and asked Dawn to look at her face. Then I asked her to try and smile. Carefully watching her own face, Dawn smiled! I cried with joy. In great excitement I was allowed to take her out into the grounds of the hospital in a wheelchair. There I was thrilled as Dawn sang the chorus,

> His name is Wonderful,
> His name is Wonderful,
> His Name is Wonderful, Jesus my Lord.
> He is the Mighty King,
> Master of Everything,
> His name is Wonderful, Jesus my Lord.

He's the great Shepherd,
The Rock of all Ages,
Almighty God is He.
His name is Wonderful,
His name is Wonderful,
His Name is Wonderful, Jesus my Lord.

It was amazing - a miracle. Who said Dawn would be a vegetable? Not our God. He had saved her and was restoring her to us, answering the prayers of his people as he had promised to do.

When Rex or I were with her, Dawn seemed to respond fairly well and the neuro-surgeon soon suggested that we take her home for a day. I was frightened, not knowing what to expect. That first visit was successful, however. She was brought on a stretcher and lay in her room, appearing calm and happy. She even started to read a book and asked if she could take the book back with her to the hospital. No sooner did she return, however, from this brief visit that she tore up the book and caused a rumpus! It was becoming obvious that hospitalization was upsetting her - she had been there for three months - so if home would help her, home she must come.

There were many frightening things which we were encountering for the first time and of which we had no experience. Dawn suffered several epileptic fits which were very distressing. In addition, as power began to return to her body her movements were all strange and muddled and she could not control them. Because she was doubly incontinent we were supplied with plastic sheeting for her bed. Often she would slide out of bed taking her bedclothes with her and would lie on the floor, giggling madly. In fact, she was beginning to giggle uncontrollably and would therefore have what we called 'accidents'. Even David, her brother who had the effect of making her laugh at the simplest 'antic' had to start being 'terribly serious' to prevent 'accidents' at the most inopportune times! Poor Dawn! I asked the doctor's advice about her giggling but he just told me to be grateful she was not crying! I felt very weak but Rex was much stronger in his faith in believing that the Lord is mighty, and we were conscious that so many people were praying for us that we seemed to receive the strength we needed as we all prepared for her homecoming.

As she progressed from stretcher to wheelchair, the physiotherapy which she had been receiving increased. It was a long, painful, daily routine. Eventually two large leg-length calipers were fitted to Dawn's legs and she tried to walk with two tripod sticks in her hands. It all caused her so much pain. She began to come home more and more, however, travelling daily to the hospital for physiotherapy until finally she was allowed to come home to stay. She would keep up her physiotherapy and be regularly monitored and she would be plagued with the problem of incontinency for a long time, but she was home with us, at last. Thankfully the problem has now gone.

My daily reading on the day of Dawn's traumatic

illness was from Hudson Taylor's book, *God's Guiding Hand* .

'My soul, wait thou only upon God' (Psalm 62:5). To most of God's children there come times of sudden awakening, when some unexpected trial, an illness, or a bereavement has revealed to us, with startling effect how, all unconsciously perhaps, our souls were not waiting 'only upon God' but were leaning on an instrument or on circumstances ... But surely, surely he should not only be our last resource; rather the first to whom we turn in our difficulties, whether they be small or great.

8
Preparing For Something

Almost a year after Dawn had became ill a letter arrived quite unexpectedly from the Officers Christian Union. It asked Rex if we would consider going to Kilravock Castle, near Croy in Inverness-shire to work as wardens and housekeepers.

We were extremely surprised at this proposal. Rex was at this time in partnership with a group of insurance brokers and we were settled in Newcastle, with our family around us. Diana had married a charming young man named Antony and they lived not far away from us. David had left home, but was nearby, having commenced training as a 'Police Cadet' in the Durham Constabulary. He came home every weekend. The request was so unusual, however, that we were intrigued to find out more about it.

It appeared that a Miss Elizabeth Rose of Kilravock, Chief of the Clan Rose, had written to the chairman of the Officer's Christian Union enquiring if they could recommend a suitable married couple to run her castle as a Christian guest house, and a hall in the castle grounds which was being built to become a conference centre. There was also an old granary (it retained its name - The Granary) which had been restored to provide residential accommodation, primarily for young people of numbers up to about forty. Miss Rose herself was travelling to Australia and was leaving three ladies to make the appointment on her behalf.

We knew absolutely nothing about guest houses but we saw it as something of a challenge and after much prayer we felt we should travel north to Scotland to find out more. Dawn, thankfully, was well enough to travel with us. When we arrived in Croy we met the three ladies to discuss the proposal. It all went very smoothly and everybody seemed to approve of everybody else. Slowly we began to see this opening as an opportunity for service and to believe that the Lord could be calling us to go north. The salary was a problem as it would be far less than half of what Rex earned as a broker but our accommodation would be covered by living in the west wing of the Castle. We went home to Newcastle to think and to pray.

Early in 1972 we returned to the Highlands. Rex had resigned from his firm and we had sold our house. We took our furniture with us and soon began to settle in to our new home and this new way of life. We were fortunate in being able to arrange for Dawn to be taken the few miles into Inverness to the Technical College where she courageously began a Secretarial Course. It was her first major venture into a world which did not know of her difficulties and we were very proud of her. David also joined us, having left the Durham Police, and whilst awaiting entry into the then Inverness-shire Constabulary helped with odd-jobs about the castle.

I cannot pretend, however, that life at the castle was happy or enjoyable. We did our best, but somehow our best was not good enough. There were times of tremendous happy fellowship amongst the guests who were most appreciative but at other times guests were difficult and unreasonable. Things did not run smoothly and we had many worries. In addition, Rex felt that the spiritual opportunities he had hoped to be able to develop were few and he felt he was unsuited to the other side of the work.

One morning sticks in my mind as being particularly difficult. I had gone down to the kitchen in the morning to discover that the cook had not arrived. No breakfast was being prepared and I hastily began to improvise, cooking sausages and bacon for each guest. David was acting as a waiter in the dining room. I recall being covered with embarrassment when I saw how small the breakfast looked on the plates. David had no such qualms and only added to my discomfort by telling the guests to cut it up into tiny pieces to make it look like more! We couldn't help but see the hilarious side much much later.

As the months wore on the trustees showed little understanding of our position. They gathered together and decided that we should leave. But where were we to go? House prices had risen alarmingly since we had sold our home to move north and what we had simply could not provide us with another home. In addition, the salary we had received had been very small indeed.

During this time Dawn also became unwell. When we called in a doctor we had to explain her past history. He was extremely discouraging, and crowned our downheartedness by leaving us with the prognosis, 'I give her ten years!'

We were in what one might call a thornbush. Every way we turned we seemed to feel its thorns pricking us. We believed we had been meant to come to Scotland - we had felt guided by God to come - but now Rex was unemployed, we were to be homeless, Dawn was disabled and the trustees had treated us with cruelty, showing a complete lack of understanding of our predicament. Even the telephone was cut off from our use. We were entirely isolated and during the winter months the castle was very cold. Miss Rose was visiting Australia during this time. I kept telling myself that God does not make mistakes but it became increasingly hard to understand. We were miserable, weak and alarmingly puzzled.

We were greatly relieved when a Christian lady kindly sent us a loan to enable us to buy a small house in Inverness. Early in the morning Rex would leave to search for somewhere for us to live and also for employment. I would be left without transport or even a telephone until he returned. I was not as strong as I should have been in waiting for God's guidance. I was very impatient and my heart ached for Rex who had to provide for us all. Eventually, however, he did find a house in Inverness and he was able to return to being a broker for employment. We hoped to be able to repay the loan as quickly as possible.

Several years later we received a letter from the chairman of the trustees and in it he expressed his sorrow at what had occurred. He asked us to forgive him for having permitted such unhappiness and unfairness. We did not know what had prompted this request but it was gratefully received. It is not easy always to forgive, perhaps especially our fellow believers, but we knew we must. Even although we knew that our own sins are not remembered by God after we are forgiven I had to search my own heart to see if I could positively answer whether or not I had stored up this difficult, trying situation as an unforgiven, bitter memory. Miss Rose herself has at all times shown us the utmost kindness, she is a lovely, fully committed Christian lady in every respect. As the years have passed gradual changes have taken place. The castle is now a beautiful place in which to stay and to enjoy a time of relaxation, comfort, warm fellowship and good food. It is a pleasure to visit and to be welcomed with loving caring eagerness to make a stay quite unique.

Although Rex had returned to his previous profession his heart was gradually urging him to a very different service. God was calling him. Many years had elapsed since Rex had been at the Bible Churchman's Missionary Society. He had been in the Regular Army for fifteen years, had been wounded several times and was much decorated. At times he had been far from God - I began to recognize that he must have been or he would never have become so friendly with me or eventually married me. I also understood his family's dislike of our marriage as I had been ignorant of what they believed in and to which they longed for Rex to return. But he had returned to God and now God was calling him into his service. Rex was now in his early fifties. He had considered an Army chaplaincy but we discovered that he was too old to apply for this. We wondered into what kind of service he could be being led.

As a family we had joined the West Parish Church in Inverness. The minister, Rev. Tom Swanston, was a fine teacher and preacher there and we benefited greatly during this time of decision, from his depth of insight and gift of bringing the Scriptures alive to his listeners. For this and for the many friends we made at the West Church I will be forever grateful.

While in Inverness I was invited to attend a Ladies Bible Study Discussion Group, held in the home of a couple who were greatly used for Christ in the Inverness area, Dr and Mrs Murchison. It was so lovely to gather with about twelve others for one morning each week. We came from many different Churches, all to share together, to study, to learn from each other and to share in prayer and fellowship. I smile as I recall those of us who possessed commentaries. We would stagger in, weighed down heavily with enormous books, such as Matthew Henry's or the IVP Bible Commentaries!

Dr. Murdoch and Maurine Murchison had a large house which was used for the Lord, and once a month a special speaker would be invited and each member of the group would bring along neighbours and friends who were not committed Christians. Some time later Maurine suggested that some of us break away and open our own homes to start new groups. This we proceeded to do and now, seventeen years later, there are sixty-seven groups.

It was as the culmination of much prayer and consideration that two of Rex's war-time friends who had become ministers in the Church of Scotland encouraged Rex to similarly apply for this ministry. An application form was completed and sent and soon Rex was requested to attend a Selection Committee for the Church of Scotland ministry. He was accepted on the condition that he would agree to attend a University Divinity Faculty for two years. His entrance into full time study would, we knew put us financially 'on the rocks' again and we were perhaps cautious after our experiences at Kilravock but God was directing us through his Word and his people. As the way had opened up for him to go we had become convinced that God was leading us and that it was our duty to follow.

In October of that year Rex began his studies at Aberdeen University. He settled in and soon he and another mature student, five years older than Rex, became known as the Grandpas of the faculty. It was not an easy transition for him, however, as every mature student will understand, entering a class of bright young students after so many years away from a studious environment: after his first term Rex returned home to us looking quite grey with the strain of having to study late in life.

He also found it very difficult when biblical authority was questioned by the lecturers and tutors. Frequently his answers were rejected on this basis and he found this terribly difficult to accept. It reminded me of one occasion when we had visited an Anglican church while still living in Newcastle. The vicar had refuted the story of Jonah and the big fish saying it could not be true. Although he had not walked out, Rex had declared that we would not listen to such heresy again. Now he was hearing similar claims from those who were instructing him as a student minister. He refused to be shaken however, holding fast to 1 Corinthians 9:16, 'Woe to me if I preach not the gospel', and II Timothy 4:2, 'Preach the word'.

Before we received a grant to assist Rex's studies, I applied for part-time employment at a school for the physically and mentally handicapped in Inverness. I had been trained in Physical Education remedial work and I found that my experiences with Dawn helped me greatly. I enjoyed this opportunity to help these children for whom so many activities and tasks were difficult or even impossible.

By this time Dawn had bravely mastered her

secretarial course and was employed by the Highland Health Board in Inverness. There were, however, continued difficulties resulting from her illness which could not be overlooked. In her office she was managing quite well and most of the staff were very kind. One little man, however sneezed quite a lot and as he was very small (and rather peculiar!) he would stand on a chair and sneeze out of the window. This to Dawn was hilariously funny but her frequent amusement was not appreciated when it caused one of her 'accidents'.

I have always been absolutely convinced that God has been watching over her and encouraging her ever since he gave her back her life and if employers and staff were baffled and confusing, then Rex or I had to rise to her assistance and explain some of the results of the damage caused during the time she was in the coma. We could see the improvements even if no-one else could. But each day was a world being regained.

It appeared that we were now emerging from our trouble - bound thornbush and we gave thanks to God for smiling upon us. Things were not going to be easy but we could now go forward, not looking back.

David now a constable in the then 'Northern Constabulary' much to our delight, was stationed in Inverness. It was lovely to have him near at hand, especially when Rex was away for these long periods of study. A burden was being laid on David at this time for his fellow policemen. Together with Christian Police friends he prayed with the ultimate view of forming a Northern Branch of the Christian Police Association (CPA), similar to those in which he had been involved in other parts of the country.

I do not know all the details but for many months discussions and correspondence were taking place. Permission had to be granted by the Chief Constable and plans made. After encouragements and upsets permission was eventually obtained for a Northern Branch to be formed and in March 1980 the inaugural meeting was held at Police Headquarters. It was a very happy, never-to-be forgotten occasion with many visiting CPA members from as far afield as Northern Ireland. I believe it was an evening which brought great glory to our Lord and it was wonderful to see David with his CPA Colleagues involved in witnessing for Jesus in this way.

At University Rex was doing well. His two years were passing quickly after the initial struggle and he greatly appreciated the studying and the companionship of the other students. He had outstandingly encouraging comments from his professors and we soon found ourselves after his two years approaching another uncertainty - What would happen now? We had become settled in Inverness but another stage in Rex's endeavour to serve Christ in this way had been reached. We prayed for the difficult task ahead of discovering where Rex would go in order to serve the Lord.

9
Called

Shortly before the conclusion of his two years at Aberdeen University Rex had been asked if he would apply for the vacancy for a church in Edinburgh. Rex had been grateful to be asked but had explained that he would prefer to be called by a church and therefore he did not apply. This was very important to him as he wanted to know the clear guidance of God in everything he did as he considered where he would become a minister. His professor's request that Rex complete an application form for St. Serf's Church of Scotland in Edinburgh was so persistent, however, that we believed that this could be God's way of directing us. Soon the papers were completed and sent away and we awaited the unfolding of God's guidance to us.

It was during the last term of his studies that a call came for Rex to preach at a church in Edinburgh where he would be heard by a Vacancy Committee. This was the usual beginning of a process by which delegates from a church heard various preachers and chose a small number, perhaps only one, to be heard by the church. Rex telephoned me after he had preached in Edinburgh, telling me that he had spoken on the Cross of Christ. Shortly afterwards I had another phone call from St. Serf's in Edinburgh asking me to make contact with my husband and to tell him that the Vacancy Committee had selected him as their sole nominee. After I had spoken to Rex and told them of the committee's decision Rex said his legs felt like cotton wool. He was apprehensive knowing that the next step would be for him to meet and preach to the church and then to meet with the elders and the deacons, if the congregation voted to call him.

His time at University completed, Rex left Aberdeen and came home. It was a time of much thought and prayer as we went over the questions that constantly presented themselves to our minds. Was the Lord really leading and guiding us to what appeared to be a fashionable church in the country's capital city? Rex had always visualized himself after ordination in a small country charge. With his relative inexperience was it wise to accept so large and prominent a church so soon after completing his theological studies? How would they respond to the various innovations we would wish to make - a prayer meeting, a mid-week Bible Study, and evening service of which we heard there had not been one for forty years? In addition, Rex had been a soldier and was very tall and handsome, he bore the title of Major, he had a soldier's bearing and had been accustomed to using his authority. He looked the part! Could all these have had some influence upon their decision to approach him as their minister to preach the gospel?

Together we would pray and talk. We daily walked around an area in Inverness by the river, known as the Ness Islands with our dogs and we discussed and prayed over these questions while we walked. Rex became increasingly sure during these days and weeks that he must go forward. He believed that doors were unexpectedly opening and that he should not hold back any longer.

I went to Edinburgh with Rex when he was called to preach to the congregation of St. Serf's. A room had been booked for us in a nearby rather sordid hotel. We were grateful that it was near the church but it was so dirty! We had to cover the chairs in the bedroom with our raincoats before we sat on them. Nobody offered us hospitality.

The following morning was the Sunday and it dawned a most glorious day. Trembling with nervousness and leaning heavily on our God we made our way to the church. Rex was in God's hands and God was in control.

It was a beautiful building. Inside, its walls were panelled with lovely light wood and a reredos of this same wood divided the choir from the congregation. My nervous thoughts as I sat right on the back pew made me imagine trapped people peeping through the spaces in the trellis work. Would the Holy Spirit give them ears to hear?

The church was full and Rex preached powerfully, the Holy Spirit truly speaking though him. I was asked to leave the church before the congregation voted but if my memory serves me correctly, I believe only four out of almost four hundred voted against. Therefore the congregation decisively chose Rex as their minister.

He then met members of the Session and after they had asked him various questions, Rex was able to put most of his own questions which we had puzzled over to the elders. Again and again they answered positively although Rex felt it wise not to request permission to restart an evening service immediately. If he was to take up this charge it would not do to ask for too much too soon!

Afterwards we were shown the Manse. It was in one of the loveliest areas in Edinburgh and had large, well-proportioned rooms and a small garden surrounding three sides of the house. It was also very solid externally but unfortunately it was in poor condition inside with no heating, and old gas brackets which had previously provided the lighting lined the walls. In addition, the previous minister had been a smoker and the walls of every room were stained with smoke. There were no carpets or floor coverings of any kind, which would mean a large outlay of money by ourselves. It did, however, have a perfectly good room which would serve as a study once a few shelves were put up.

With plans chasing round our heads, back we travelled to Inverness to discuss it with our family. Together we planned and prayed about each stage. Our church family entered enthusiastically into prayer with us.

Rex had asked his evangelical friends for more

information about the church but nobody appeared to know much, or if they did, they preferred not to say. One shock was to hear that St. Serf's held a theatre licence and ran a very popular and active Drama Club. It was apparently greatly admired in the city and was counted on to provide a fine income.

This was very strange to us and we were confused both as to how to account for this in a church and also as to how we would tackle this situation if we were to go. By this stage Rex had been selected and called by the congregation and we had reached the position where we had to decide whether or not we should go.

I can still hear myself saying to Rex, 'Do you really believe that this is the right place for you? Is this the right time to make this move? Are you sure, really sure that this is God's desire for you?'

To each question Rex gave the same answer, 'Yes, Yes, Yes!'

10
Minister's Wife

In the hot summer of 1976 the time came for us to leave our church family in Inverness. Rex had been licensed in the West Church in Inverness to enter the ministry and soon afterwards we said our goodbyes to them and set off for our new home in Edinburgh. When we left they presented us with a beautiful clock, giving a miniature one to Dawn. We were sorry to leave so many friends behind. We had no relatives or friends in Edinburgh and were aware that it might be quite lonely for us initially, although we hoped that we would soon settle.

We sold our house in Inverness. It was a little like a biscuit tin compared to the large manse waiting for us and we knew that our tiny carpets and meagre furniture would be useless in our new home. The house sale, however, paid for the carpeting and we also bought a cheap car as Rex would be expected to visit the many hospitals in Edinburgh as part of his pastoral work.

When we arrived we were grateful to find that the congregation of St. Serf's had assisted us by modernizing the kitchen a little and most of the rooms had been repainted. Much had still to be done but it was understandable that they would not be able to finance all that was required. During the hot, sticky weather we moved into our new manse, rattling around in the many rooms and trying to make our furniture, such as it was, occupy at least some of them.

Our first meeting with the congregation of St. Serf's would be at Rex's induction service and arrangements were going ahead for this event. When it arrived, friends came from all over the United Kingdom and we appreciated their encouragement at the start of this service for the Lord. The service itself was a very moving occasion and it was wonderful to be a part of the solemnity and simplicity with which we were charged to begin our work. My husband's ministry had begun and I had vowed to support him through every moment of every day. Our desire was to love these people and we were enthusiastic to see men and women and children coming to know Jesus as Saviour and Lord.

On the following evening the congregation provided a 'Welcoming Social' for us. As we were comparatively new to the Church of Scotland we had no real idea what form this might take. I had rarely witnessed an Induction Service: a Church of Scotland 'Social' made me wonder what to expect or how to behave. It was with some nervousness that we arrived and we were ushered into the Church's palatial halls.

Many people were there including other ministers from the city. The congregation itself was large and we were also to be introduced to the Drama Club of which so many of the congregation were members.

To commence the evening, the choir sang several pieces, including, 'Three little maids from school ....' from *The Mikado*; 'Getting to know you ....' from *The King and I*, and 'Sunrise, sunset ....' from *Fiddler on the Roof*. All were secular pieces and the fact that we were seated in the 'Theatre' which was well known in Edinburgh and used regularly by the city's festival, as well as the sight of tables filled with bottles of wine for our refreshment struck such a discordant note with the holy vows and prayerful solemnity of the previous evening that we were quite taken aback. We tried not to show our surprise and soon several speeches followed, one on behalf of local ministers, and the President of the Women's Guild made the official presentation of robes.

We soon discovered that many members of the congregation were extremely kind and eager to be involved. Many of them gave much of their spare time to the numerous church activities: the Drama Club, a Badminton Club, a large Women's Guild, Guides, Choir, Coffee Mornings and various Sales of Work. In addition, many members of the church were faithfully committed to collecting some disabled folk from a nearby Cheshire Home and bringing them to church. They would sit with them and give them any help which was necessary.

There was also a Sunday School in which some of the members taught. It took place during the service on Sunday when they and the children left the church after a short children's talk.

Amongst all this activity, however, there was only one service for worship, teaching and fellowship each week, on Sunday from 11 am to 12 noon. There was no evening service, no meeting for prayer or for Bible Study. We were extremely puzzled by all this and we soon realised that the members fully expected their new and inexperienced minister to conform to all the practices and methods used over the years.

One of our first concerns was for Dawn. Our daughter had left her job in Inverness but we still realised how important it was for her to be occupied. But we also knew that finding a suitable post for her could be difficult. The Disablement Resettlement Officer responsible for the part of Edinburgh in which we lived was a most understanding and helpful person. Nothing was too much trouble for her. She searched and visited employers until she found part-time employment for Dawn and this was a great help to us. Later, Dawn applied for a vacancy as a typist at the Police Headquarters in Fettes Avenuc which also proved successful and she was very happy there.

Every morning Rex would get up at 6.00 am. He would have a cold bath, shave and dress and then go down to his study to have his 'quiet time'. He always started his day like this and I was learning to follow him in my own Bible Study and in regular prayer times. I found myself not only resting in God as I had done before but also feeding and learning from him too, discovering that if I remained in him I grew strong as his strength became mine. Rex regularly disciplined his own life in this way as well as advocating it to others - and submitting to this early morning programme had the added advantage that he brought tea upstairs for us before I got up!

I cannot recall all of Rex's sermons but he began his preaching ministry by speaking on the basics of the faith: Christ's Person; Man's Need; Christ's Work and Man's Response; Salvation and Repentance. During these sermons we noticed that nobody brought or used a Bible. It seemed to be alien to them to think of using one. And Rex's subjects seemed to be unacceptable too: they were 'too strong for their liking'. It was difficult to know where to begin as they were obviously so lost, never having been taught the truth about Christ. One Sunday, I heard two ladies behind me talking before the service began. One said to the other, 'I wonder what he will say today that we will disagree with.' Her companion replied, 'Well, I have thought quite a lot about all he said last week about heaven and hell. Most unusual!'

We soon became aware that many members of the church were dissatisfied with their new minister. We did not want to change anything too quickly but Rex would only preach what he believed and nothing could alter that. Why, oh why, I asked had they chosen my beloved husband if they did not believe what he held to be true?

When Rex met with the Sunday School teachers,

he spoke to them gently regarding the problem of leaving the service to teach the children when no other opportunity was available for them to attend a complete service. Their reaction was immediately hostile. They claimed that the situation had satisfied their previous minister for years and they did not intend to change. They were not pleased and started to leave the church.

Soon an elder resigned his post having taken offence at Rex's request for him not to smoke his pipe during meetings of the Kirk Session. Rex had been very careful to approach this man privately and in a kindly manner but to no avail. This elder was such a good man and his attitude was very upsetting.

Wise evangelical friends of ours advised Rex to go slowly. We did not wish to offend and he did try so hard to be gentle. We knew that God had guided us here and we held on to our belief that God did not make mistakes.

Problems were soon encountered, however, over the Drama Club. As it was of the utmost importance to its members, Rex said nothing about it, but he felt he could not attend their performances. They were all secular plays and sometimes the choice of material performed was not even seemly or the language particularly pure. The lack of attendance by their minister did not please the members who felt that Rex should support their performances and they made their dissatisfaction known to all.

From the Women's Guild also, we sensed confusion and opposition. The Women's Guild is usually the ladies' meeting in the Church of Scotland and once a year the Minister is invited to speak at it. When the time came, Rex was asked to take part. At the end of Rex's talk he asked the ladies if they had any questions. One lady stood up: 'Mr Beatty,' she said, 'you are always talking about sin. I have known all these ladies for many years and I want you to know that none of them are sinners!'

I listened to Rex's gentle reply in which he explained why we are all sinners, but they would not agree and, I fear, were greatly offended.

We were very much aware of this growing hostility. We also were very aware of our own failings. We needed to pray for ourselves. God had given so many promises: what must we do to experience them? We prayed that we might cling to them in faith: 'Be strong - and work, for I am with you' (Haggai 2:4) How we prayed that we would be able to do so. We knew we had put our hand to the task and could not look back.

During this time we attended Holyrood Abbey Church of Scotland on Sunday evenings as Rex had held back from requesting that an evening service be held in St. Serf's. At Holyrood, we were made very welcome and found kindred spirits with a great many in the congregation. We also enjoyed the preaching and teaching of Rev. James Philip and valued his friendship and counsel as we came to know him.

We also met Hugh and Margaret Miller there. Hugh was a farmer and they had three sons who were also farmers and their daughter was a nurse with the South American Mission serving in Brazil. We soon became very friendly with them - Hugh and Rex discovered their mutual interest in eschatology and we frequently visited their farm, usually on a Monday which was our free day. We were so very grateful to the Miller family who showed us such kindness and shared our concerns and we remained friends for years. They prayed with us, sharing the delights and encouraging us during the most upsetting and difficult days.

It was becoming known locally that the new minister at St. Serf's was preaching the Bible and new faces started to appear. This was so encouraging as until this time we had only been aware of a depletion rather than a growth in numbers of those attending the service. In addition, the Bible Study and Prayer Meeting which had begun with only Rex, Dawn and myself was slowly being frequented by some of the newcomers. A few of the congregation had gathered but excused themselves to practice with the Drama Club and gradually they had stopped coming but the newcomers to the church remained.

Sadly, however, we were increasingly aware that the congregation was divided. There were those for whom social activities and sales were all important, and those who chose to attend the Bible Study and Prayer Meetings. We became known as the 'Holy Huddle' and any attempt to bridge the gap between these two groups only appeared to broaden it. Rex did not condemn the social activities but he felt he could not support many of them. He had become known as a 'hard liner', which in some respects was true as he could not compromise his beliefs. He knew that God's Word had to be obeyed. But we had not expected serving God would be such a battle. I remember Rex saying that it was more difficult to be a soldier in the army of Christ than a soldier in the regular Army!

Some months after we arrived Rex decided to begin preaching systematically from the beginning of the Bible. In addition, he urged people to bring their own Bibles to enable them to follow and to see that he was preaching not merely his own personal opinion but rather that which God had written and given to us all.

One morning some weeks after Rex had begun this series of sermons we had a visitor. It was a member of the Kirk Session, an ordained minister who lectured at New College in Old Testament History. He asked to see Rex.

He did not stay long. After he had left, Rex was obviously upset and he told me that his visitor had called to inform him that he was leaving the church. His reason, he told Rex, was that Rex was preaching from the book of Genesis as if he believed it to be true! This lecturer said that it could not be true, indeed he knew it was not, as he visited Israel every year to study, this was his area of knowledge and, in addition, his archeological research upheld his point of view. Nothing could persuade him otherwise.

It was extremely sad and proved to be the catalyst for other departures. Once it was known that an ordained minister, indeed a lecturer at the Church of Scotland's own college was leaving, many followed. Great gaps appeared in the church and the Sunday School became very small too.

Tensions mounted in the congregation. The Kirk Session were up in arms against Rex. Nobody wanted to fill the empty spaces left by resigning elders: they were frightened and admitted as much. More disagreements had arisen about sending a special offering of money to a missionary association and eventually after seven months in St. Serf's the session reported Rex to the Edinburgh Presbytery as being incompatible with part of the congregation.

Their main and most immediate grievance was over an Ecumenical Service which was due to take place as being the custom amongst several churches in the area. It had not been mentioned to Rex by the Vacancy Committee or anyone else and we knew nothing of it until the arranged programme was prepared. It was an extremely difficult situation as it involved participating in a service with a Roman Catholic priest and Rex could not agree to this. He was immediately accused of being anti-Roman Catholic, extreme and intolerant.

The local and national newspapers published the story with varying degrees of accuracy but many exaggerated the situation grossly. These reports only seemed to intensify the situation and during this time a secret meeting of the Kirk Session was held with a member of the Edinburgh Presbytery in the Scout

Hut - without Rex even being informed!

The accusations hurled at Rex were particularly painful both because we felt we had treaded so carefully and also because we had Roman Catholic friends in Edinburgh. The kindest person on our arrival in the city was, in fact, a Roman Catholic lady living opposite us in Denham Green Terrace. She invited us to join her for a meal on the day we moved into the manse and she remained a most friendly person at all times throughout the years.

It was an extremely unfortunate situation. Suddenly the eye of the Presbytery and of the Church of Scotland as a whole and even of the nation through the popular press was turned upon us. Poor Rex was in deep trouble. Giants on every side crowding in trying to take control of God's house. We knew that there are no limits set to the power of God and we prayed for wisdom and guidance but the stress and pressure were continually there. He was facing a tragic situation in which there could be no winners, only losers. When he was called before the Edinburgh Presbytery he therefore reluctantly agreed to leave if called to another suitable congregation.

Following this a church in the Black Isle, north of Inverness, did invite Rex to preach. After hearing him they did call him to become their minister but the manse was very isolated, as well as large, making it impossible for Dawn to be employed. We decided to return to Edinburgh and if the situation was relieved at all we would continue in the work given to us by the Lord, winning souls for Jesus

Christ where the Lord had sent us. It was not an easy decision to make.

We knew that we were re-entering a 'them and us' situation with the 'them' contingent strong and vociferous in their claims that we had spoilt not only their fun and amusement but had also ruined their church. But the prophet, Isaiah, promised that 'when you pass through the waters .... they will not sweep over you' (43:2) and we felt we had to face this opposition with the claims of Jesus and cling to God's promises again and again. Thus, we returned and with the support of some, continued our service there.

To help Rex I started to make door - to - door visits in the tenement flats near the church. It was the start of outreach work which would produce small but precious results. I met an attractive young woman with two young children in one flat. I was warmly greeted and invited into her home. We chatted very happily and I asked if this young mother would like to visit the church which she could almost see from her window and also if she would like her children to attend Sunday School.

These suggestions were met with much enthusiasm and pleasure and she told me that nobody had ever called on her from any church. Rex also visited and soon Lynn came to church and her children to Sunday School. She explained that her husband was a Roman Catholic and he was not at all pleased about her becoming interested in church but her interest grew and grew until she could do no other than give her life to Jesus. She was radiant in her new life but it had been a brave step as her husband was very displeased. He would not speak to us and refused admission to Rex when he called at their flat.

Our Prayer Meeting had been growing and we brought Peter, Lynn's husband to the Lord in prayer. Six weeks later we were thrilled when Lynn brought her husband to the manse to ask for counselling to become a Christian. Later Peter was baptised and to this day the family continue to grow and witness for the Lord.

By this time the original Sunday School teachers had departed and had been replaced by others including Dawn and myself. We began with twelve children. After visiting all the surrounding houses and local schools more children started to attend until our Primary section grew to eighty children. This was a real sign to us of God's continuing presence and provision and it gave Rex great opportunities for visiting the homes of these children and meeting their parents.

One of those who sent her daughter to Sunday School was Ivy. Ivy, however, refused to attend the church herself as she said she was a communist and did not consider Jesus Christ to be the Son of God. Rex and I both felt particularly drawn to Ivy and her husband whose strong opinions made them furious at being challenged. We often met as we lived in the same area and had many useful discussions together.

A young married nurse began attending the church.

Her husband sailed with the Merchant Navy, so Mary was often by herself. She was converted and became one of a growing number of newly committed Christians in St. Serf's. When Mary's husband came home on leave he was not really interested in what he called 'this being born again business' but he came to church with her occasionally. Every time he went back to sea, Mary packed a Bible into his case. Her persistence was rewarded as this man has now come to Christ.

During those early years others too believed: a blind lady in the church; an ex-alcoholic who was wonderfully converted and developed a fine witness; a businessman in the city. Together we grew stronger in faith and love as a family of believers.

Our son David by this time had been stationed on Skye. He later left the Police for a period of Bible Training at what is now Northumbria Bible College. After a year he re-entered the Northern Constabulary and was stationed on the remote Hebridean islands of Barra and Benbecula. We saw him on each and every leave he had, but we were especially delighted when he arrived at the manse one day with a quiet young Christian girl from Skye, called Ishbel - his fiancee. She was a nurse and after their wedding some time later on the Isle of Skye they lived in Dingwall. There they both lived until David left the police to enter the full-time ministry of the United Free Church of Scotland.

As the day to day work of the parish settled down, Rex obtained the approval of the Kirk Session to commence a Sunday evening service for his depleted congregation. It was a great breakthrough and something we had hoped to begin for a long time although it meant the end of our happy evenings at Holyrood Abbey. Many said they would attend, but over the years the normal congregation only numbered between fifteen and twenty.

On one occasion there were several more, however. In the afternoon, between the Sunday services, Rex would try and rest and sometimes slept. One Sunday he joined us for tea saying that he had just had a clear dream that there would be thirty-four present at the evening service. That night the usual Christians were there. Just as Rex appeared, in came a number of Faith Mission students from their Bible College in Edinburgh. We did not know why they had chosen that night to attend but on that evening the total congregation numbered thirty-four.

The most outstanding and wonderful miracle about the evening service was the offering. It was as if the Lord had put his own hand into the offering at each evening service. Sometimes there were bundles of notes totalling over £100.00. The Treasurer who was never at the service could not understand. Although numbers were very low the financial contribution was unbelievably and outstandingly good. We gave our thanks to God who was transforming trials into blessings, by surrounding them and those of us involved with his love and grace.

The gospel of Christ has a remarkable effect upon people - positive and negative. There have always been those who would die for Christ and others who are angered by the message. The congregation of St. Serf's were such upright, kind and self-sufficient people. They just wanted to be happy and good. They did not really want to learn or study God's Word. Many had never previously encountered the truth that Jesus demands repentance and absolute trust from his people. And when they did hear it from their minister many chose to be angry, the negative effect. Some, however, chose the other way, truly becoming disciples of Christ and we rejoiced that this change was gradually, painfully taking place.

11
Numbered Days

Six years into his ministry at St Serf's, Rex was as busy as ever. Almost every evening he would go out visiting in the parish, anxious to bring those both in the congregation and who lived in the vicinity of the church to know Christ as Saviour. He was always working, studying, preparing, making new contacts, and visiting hospitals and shut-ins but it was not a chore to him. He merely felt that there was no time to waste. He knew what God had given him to do and he was going to do it.

At times, Rex looked very tired and he was prone to a nagging and persistent backache. Our doctor suggested that it might be rheumatism resulting from war wounds which Rex had received and he prescribed pain killers which my husband carried with him everywhere in his pockets. We wondered ourselves whether the pressure upon him could be aggravating the backache as we were always aware of the strain he was under.

For some time I had myself been suffering from a painful hip which was diagnosed as arthritis. It was not deemed critical enough for surgery although I eventually received regular physiotherapy, so I limped around using a stick. Sitting on the hard pews in church was very painful and I carried a cushion around with me to make it more comfortable. The three of us, Dawn, Rex and I, must have looked like real crocks; Dawn with two sticks, me with one, and Rex's upright bearing often stiffened with cramp in his back!

But he soldiered on. Some progress was seen in that two hundred Bibles were bought for the church and gradually the rustling of pages could be heard as the congregation followed the readings and preaching. In addition, new people were joining the church and there was a growing number of converted people. Slowly, attendance at the midweek Bible Study and Prayer Meeting had increased and we enjoyed fellowship with these lovely Christians who were standing against popular opinion in supporting us. But it was said of Rex that he lived what he preached and he was at least respected for this by some of his opponents. Indeed, I believe that many loved him, like one dear old lady who told me that 'the minister calls, you know, and always insists on making *me* a cup of tea,' but they were often frightened of making their fondness of him known.

As Rex's nagging backache continued, we were glad to be able to take our holiday that summer. During the months of July and August St. Serf's regularly joined with another Church of Scotland in the area worshipping for a month in the other building and a month in our own. This allowed both ministers to take their holidays without having to call upon extra holiday replacements. Our doctor had suggested that a virus was causing Rex's trouble and we enjoyed our holiday as a means of giving Rex a rest from the continual activity.

There was an added benefit from this brief union of congregations in that a young man from our neighbouring church was converted. Leaving the church one morning this young solicitor had spoken to Rex at the door and asked if he could come to a service at our own church. After he came he believed and he joined us in St. Serf's and was a great help and encouragement to us all.

One day when Rex met me after my physiotherapy session at the hospital he told me that he had been to see our doctor again. For some time he had been suffering agonizing cramp at night and had been finding it difficult to get relief from this although his quinine tablets had helped a little. Dark rings surrounded his eyes and it was with some relief as well as anxiety that Rex said the doctor had advised a spell in hospital to undergo some tests.

Rex was quickly given a date to enter hospital and the tests began. We did not know how long it would take but I knew something was seriously wrong when our doctor, who lived a few doors away from us, called at the manse after only the third day of investigations. He was an excellent man and a caring doctor and he told me quickly what had been discovered: Rex had a malignant tumour in his spine and had advanced bone cancer. Our doctor wanted me to know before going to visit Rex.

I went quickly to the hospital using all the self-control I could muster in my trembling limbs and asking God to give me courage so as not to appear as frightened as I felt. But Rex was smiling at me from his bed. I smiled back with eyes clouded by tears. We had always been open and honest with each other - never secretive. I just hugged him and said, 'I know, darling, I know. The doctor has told me.'

It is difficult to describe Rex's feelings. I believe the pain over the past months had concerned him far more than he had admitted, so perhaps it was almost a relief to know the reason. How he must have suffered for a long time. I could do nothing but just look at him and love him. He did not complain or grumble. He said that God was very close and he felt very calm.

There was to be an operation on the next day. David arranged to fly from Orkney, where he was a pastor, to Edinburgh to be with me. 'Oh God,' I prayed, 'you tell me not to fear because you are with me, not to be dismayed because you are my God. You were with him - you must have been, for him to have endured the pain amongst all the troubles of the ministry. Lord,' I pleaded, 'please give me the strength and courage I need to help him now.'

The operation was unpleasant and the subsequent treatment more so. When David and I spoke to the consultant he showed us the X-rays of Rex's back. We clearly saw the tumour which showed up very dark and the grey cancer cells which covered him right through to the top of his spine and throughout his whole body. We asked for the prognosis: 'At most, six months!'

After his treatment Rex came home to the manse much thinner and weaker. But he tried to walk with his head up as he smiled to those who saw him come home. Inside, weakness overcame him and we put him quickly to bed. He suffered much discomfort and pain but he was determined to return to the pulpit and preach for as long as the Lord would allow. We could not ignorc the seriousness of the days to come or deny that they were limited but he wanted so much to continue each day as normally as possible that I felt it was my loving duty, as it was my greatest desire, to help him.

During that time the Holy Spirit filled Rex with such gracious urgency that it was inspiring to everyone. The years of rejection, subtle persecution and unkindness were in the past and forgotten. How could we let that mar our joy when every day was so precious? One of the real blessings to be given us at this time was a request by many of the women to begin an afternoon meeting. We started this fellowship in the manse and many women came and we found that it was much appreciated, meeting the needs of many. I would arrange to have a speaker and at the end we would have some tea and a time of sharing together. I loved these ladies and continue to hear from many of them. It proved to be very successful and soon the group grew so large that we had to move into the church halls to accommodate us all.

It was extremely difficult, however, for Rex to continue with his work. Visiting the vast area he had previously covered was now too great for his failing strength and increasing pain. He even began to find climbing the pulpit steps too much for him. For a time during this period, Mr Philip, minister of Holyrood Abbey Church of Scotland, kindly gave permission for his young assistant to be released to help Rex with the visiting and the midweek meetings. This was a great help, allowing Rex more time in which to rest.

David and Ishbel visited us on every leave and at every available and needful opportunity from their home in Orkney, where David was pastor to the Dounby United Free Church congregation.

It was again a traumatic time especially for father and son, as the illness progressed and the periods came to part from one another. Each was subconsciously aware of deep emotions tied up with each passing visit, both so aware of the general prognosis and the geographic separation brought about by their particular ministries.

One day of parting I do especially recall. I do not know all the details that passed between them that afternoon as David left to return to Orkney. But it was a day of tears, of deep brokenness and pathos in which, in the salty tears and in their parting embrace there was epitomised the depths ' when words are no longer sufficient' to express the love between two men-father and son. I too was broken and remain so as I remember and visualise the amazing power of the Holy Spirit's love which came down upon these precious men of mine.

As time passed, friends from Inverness and further afield came to visit us and great love and kindness was showered upon us. Missionaries home on furlough and others whom we had prayed for over the years came to visit and some even preached for Rex at the church.

As a family we had long been friendly with Rev. Colin Peckham and his wife, Mary, who had worked, before her marriage, with the Faith Mission. Colin was the Principal of a Theological Seminary in South Africa but had been invited by the Faith Mission to become the Principal of their Bible College in Edinburgh. After months of prayer the Peckhams agreed to come to Scotland.

It was the Lord's provision for us that Colin, Mary and their three children arrived in Edinburgh when they did. As soon as they arrived these two friends who were both very well-known and outstanding spokespeople for the gospel, set about to help us. Colin became a very welcome helper to us and a wonderfully gracious and understanding visitor for Rex, and Mary was a great support to me.

After one visit Colin came to me saying that sadly he was not able to give me a hopeful message from the Lord for healing for Rex. A few days later, however, two American visitors arrived at the manse and asked if they could visit Rex. I invited them to the bedroom where Rex was lying and these visitors asked if all members of the family present would gather.

I do not remember their names, they may have been very well - known but immediately one of them began to preach most movingly and with commanding authority. The whole room and everyone in it was charged with an atmosphere and presence we had never experienced before. We were all in tears and emotionally upset. The speaker then put his hands on Rex saying, 'Brother, tomorrow there will be no tumour. It will be gone. The cancer will be cured and you will be healed.' The visitors then left. Sadly, however, there was no healing.

Another visitor for Rex was a newly converted elder in the congregation of St. Serf's. Although the majority had rejected God's truth, there were some who had turned to Christ and we were so thankful for them. Rex's visitor however was rather downhearted, missing Rex's guidance and teaching, so together they encouraged one another, making a list of all the members who had come to know the Lord in a personal way in recent years. It was wonderful to see that Rex could still be used by God and given such strength and enthusiasm to go on even when he was physically so weak.

For as time passed - six months, then a year - Rex's condition worsened. The discomfort he suffered at night was particularly upsetting - although he was always more worried for me than for himself. He even moved into another bedroom so as not to disturb me. I would creep out of our room and peep in to see if he needed anything at all. He did not see me.

More often than not he was sitting up in bed: he found that the pain was more bearable sitting than lying down.

I longed to tempt him with his favourite foods as I saw him getting thinner and weaker, but he said he could always taste burnt toast. He loved trout so I cooked a trout most carefully for him. He tried so hard to please me but a few mouthfuls was all he could manage.

Because I was becoming crippled by arthritis, Rex wanted me to sell our car and get an automatic for me to drive. My hip was much worse but what was that to Rex's illness? We would laugh together and swallow our pain-killers. Happily, the Lord provided for Diana and Antony to visit us at this time and my son-in-law busily involved himself visiting garages, never resting until he discovered an automatic 'mini' for sale. Within days it was ours and Rex dragged himself to the bedroom window to watch me driving it. Again his concern was for me - not himself.

Once while out in the car, visiting our friends, the Millers, Rex turned to me almost casually saying, 'When the time comes, Jilly, I would like Jim (Rev. Philip from Holyrood Abbey) and Tom (our minister in Inverness) to conduct my funeral.' That was all he said. A great burning lump rose in my throat and for some time we drove on in silence.

It was very important for me to be brave during these months. If I did not lean upon the Lord for his strength I would be frightened and I would be useless to help Rex and also to comfort Dawn. The years in the Army had taught me a great deal about self-control and also about fear. I had been afraid when Dawn was in the coma: then Rex had been my strength. Now during this long and painful bone cancer the Lord was our great strength. But I was still, at times, afraid. I would sit by his side on his bed. We played Scrabble together and talked and shared our Bible readings but when I was alone I was worried. Sad and miserable, I knew the days were numbered.

The MacMillan nurse began calling every day and as the medicines and injections increased, Rex wrote his last parish newsletter to the congregation of St. Serf's:

> Dear Friends,
>
> It was with much anticipation that I looked forward to being with you at the recent Baptism of Eric and Mary Davidson's son. However, this was not to be, and we realise more fully when we hand over every facet of our lives to the Lord, that we accept and bow to his will and his wiser plans in everything.
>
> Most of you already know that it was eighteen months ago that I learnt that I had cancer. Coming to terms with a cancer of the bones is no easy matter. Humanly and medically it is a terminal illness. I handed my life to the Lord many years ago, and desired to do his work and to serve him.
>
> To accept that physically I am now unable to

preach, visit or study, or do the work I so love, and to personally face the possibility of going to Heaven and to be with the Lord, leaving my most beloved wife and family, who are so precious, but having preached and discussed Eternal Life after death in both pulpit and many homes, it is the putting into reality, and the testing of my faith which are the issues I now face by day and most of the night. The hours in the middle of the night are at times very long, but they are hours which I have treasured and pray that I will continue to treasure, as one is brought closer to God, in this vitally new experience. Hebrews 13:5: 'I will never leave thee nor forsake thee'.

This may give you a little understanding as to why I depend so much on your Prayers, particularly for my wife and family, and perhaps, a little selfishly, for myself, because God is not limited, since He is the God of the impossible, and HE IS OUR GOD.

Yours affectionately
Rex Beatty

It soon became obvious that for Rex's sake to relieve his pain he should go into St. Columba's Hospice which was only five minutes walk away from the manse. He went in initially for a few days of tests but his time there lengthened as he became increasingly unwell.

Being so close to home I was able to spend most of each day with Rex. I would go to the chapel service there at 10.00 am and then stay with Rex all day. As the pain was more effectively controlled in the Hospice we were able to enjoy this time together more and Rex also wasted no time and began witnessing to the other patients in his ward. There were five other men there and when he and they had the strength, Rex would talk to them about eternal life. Hearing a dying man talking about new life made these fellow sufferers listen and Rex's words gave some of them new hope.

In the bed opposite Rex was a retired headmaster who also had cancer of the spine and this man dwelt carefully on what Rex told them all. One evening as those of our family in Edinburgh gathered round Rex's bed for prayers as usual, this gentleman beckoned me over. When I went to him he simply asked, 'What are you saying to each other?' I told him that we were praying and praising God for the day and asking for his help and comfort and nearness to all of us during the night. The man replied, 'I have never prayed. Tell me, please how to pray, tell me what to say.' As I told him about Jesus and the forgiveness he offers this man's tears dampened his pillow. He nodded when I asked him if he believed that Jesus was the Son of God and again when I asked if he needed to ask Jesus to forgive his sins. Then we 'talked to Jesus as a friend' and the following night this man told me with a smile on his face that he had prayed. He had not long to live.

One of the doctors in the hospice asked Rex what he most wanted. Without hesitation he replied, 'To glorify God,' and this he endeavoured to do even in his last few weeks.

For time was running out for us. Rex had come home for Easter but the pain was so hard for him to bear that the hospice sent an ambulance for him to return. Nobody heard him complain but the pain was clearly agonising. It was with heavy hearts that we wrapped this darling man in a blanket and watched him carried back to the hospice again where we were relieved to know they could control the pain far better than was possible at home. The consultant could not say how long Rex had. I understood that only God knew but it was time for David to come from Orkney and Diana from Kent.

During those days I visited the hospice with my heart pleading with God to give me the courage to appear able to accept what was happening. I am not a brave person, perhaps appearing more in control than I know myself to be, for inwardly I was in turmoil, and misery raged.

Looking at Rex I could see his heart was filled with love for Christ. He was not afraid and knew where he was going. I also knew he loved me too - that strange dual love for Jesus and myself which had puzzled me for so long. In Rex's increasing weakness and inability to express his thoughts he sought to comfort me as his mouth kept forming the words, 'I love you, I love you.'

I stood at the foot of his bed one night before leaving and witnessed a pale aura of light surrounding him. Looking at him lying there, unable to move,

I thought of Jesus. How the Son of God must have suffered on the cross, not only a terrible, cruel death but also rejected by almost everyone. This was the loving Jesus who had brought us together and given us thirty-two years of a wonderful marriage full of love, companionship and understanding. I could find no words to express my prayerful thanks. As I stood there that night I was supremely aware of the Holy Spirit displaying his power through Rex, his servant, and with these thoughts I whispered 'goodnight' and left.

I read later that night the verse in Luke 22:43: 'And there appeared an angel unto him from heaven, strengthening him' - that was the verse.

Rex's last letters written in hospital and then in the hospice were first of all deeply spiritual, full of thanksgiving for the Lord's goodness, and secondly, full of the love and gratitude he had for the beauty and steadfast love of our marriage. The whole family and many kind friends were glad to be able to visit and be with him, including Rev. Philip and Rev. Aitken who were our neighbouring ministers in Edinburgh. All seemed to grasp something of the holiness which Rex displayed at this time.

David stayed all night with his father on one occasion and he spoke of this holiness. He was so pleased that he could be with his father and was prepared to do any small service he could. His father also shared with him that night that the Lord had permitted him in a dream a very vivid glimpse of heaven, but had gently said to him 'not quite yet'. When David asked him to describe heaven, he had said 'it was indescribable,' it could not be put into words.

Saturday, 7th, May dawned a most glorious day. As usual I went to the chapel and then to Rex in his ward: at all times he had chosen to stay with the other patients rather than take a private room. Rev. James Philip called in and we prayed together. Rex had been unable to move for a few days but his blue eyes smiled up at his friend and fellow-worker.

Dawn, David, Diana and I were with him as he quietly slipped into a coma. As the hours passed Dawn went to join the others away from the ward but David, Diana and I stayed by the bed watching every breath until at 10.00 pm my precious Rex breathed his last breath. All the other patients were crying and grieving with us as we left the ward.

'My Saviour has my treasure, and he will walk with me.'

12
Grief

For the next few days the manse was filled with people. I remember so many calling, comforting us, advising us and preparing for the funeral. David and Antony were making arrangements for it and I was grateful to have this task taken from me. The Presbytery Clerk to the Edinburgh churches had called to see me and very gently explained that on the death of a minister, the Presbytery normally made the arrangements and conducted the service. I had thanked him but repeated Rex's wishes to him that his friends should conduct the funeral and that that was our plan. I was quite innocent of acting unconventionally and had no wish other than to have our friends taking part in this most personal and private of services.

During those days many newspapers requested permission to print stories, possibly as a result of our previous unfortunate inclusion in their columns but we declined. Anything so public could only be unwanted at this time and we only inserted the death announcement and funeral details.

I will always be grateful to our friends for holding

Rex's funeral in the way in which they did. Both are godly and loving ministers and their simple participation made it a beautiful service and just how Rex would have wished. Another service was arranged for Inverness where Rex's body was to be buried and although this was what we had always planned, I found the strain of attending both these occasions very trying. There is also the custom in Scotland for the bereaved family to stand at the church door after a funeral service to thank those who have attended. This convention, however, the family and I had no desire or, I think, ability to keep either in Edinburgh or in Inverness although we were most grateful to all those who had so kindly shown their respect and concern in coming to be with us at these services. Many attended, even the Pakistani family who ran a shop near the manse which they closed during the service as a mark of respect - a lovely tribute.

Grief, I found, is an extremely multi-faceted emotion and the family all responded very differently: Diana, reserved and contained; Dawn, bewildered and unable to express the feelings she had, and David, broken in his heart. David had come with me to the hospice on the day after Rex's death. We had stood together by Rex's body which he seemed to have left very peacefully and I had been comforted. But my heart ached for my son. He is so like his father - an upright, loving man full of integrity in serving and living for his Lord. He was broken with grief.

What of myself? I do not know. For so long I felt just nothing, like a different, vague person, nothing distinct, everything bewildering. I think I must have appeared quite aloof and apart from everyone. I was not depressed, just absent from myself. I did not love God less or ask, 'Why, when all your servant wanted was to serve you where we are?' God knew the right time and took him. I clung to 2 Corinthians 12:9 'My grace is sufficient for thee: for my strength is made perfect in weakness.' Never had it seemed so real.

A mature Christian friend helped me at this time with a few words. She said, 'Rex would not wish to come back, even if he had the choice.' These were hard to hear but it was good to be told the truth and it did help to think of his joy. Others came and merely showed their love by putting their arms around me and sobbing. It meant so much - the loving and sharing. One of the first to do so and to comfort me in this way was Ivy, one of our 'door-to- door' contacts. She had recently been saved and was an exuberant, joyful young convert yet she understood my pain more sympathetically than perhaps many other older and wiser Christians.

I needed to pray. 'Lord,' I pleaded, 'I am not good at holding fast and leaning on you. It seems as if I have always had to fight back. Now I can't, Lord. Help me to remember your promises please, and to prove them, counting the good things and not dwelling on all the hurts and sorrows.' After the strain and battling of our years in Edinburgh, my heart was very sore.

It was so hard, and still is. I had experienced grief

after the death of my mother, my youngest brother, my very close friend who was murdered in Palestine, and then my father who had died after a long illness while we were in Newcastle. The grief of Rex leaving me, however, is a deep, deep physical pain which goes on and on and on.

The days and weeks which followed were bewildering at times. Nothing was distinct and vaguely I was aware of many kind people making helpful suggestions, but I could not respond. Each day was hard - such a struggle trying to get to grips with myself just to maintain a fair and sensible outlook.

I knew God did not ever make mistakes. Rex was with the Lord, but, oh, I wanted him as well. But - I also had our Lord, and my much loved daughter was also with me. For her sake as well as my own Christian witness and the answered prayers of those who shared my grief, I am grateful to the Lord for the strength only he could supply.

The family soon returned to their own homes and Dawn and I remained in the manse. We were told there was no hurry to move away. Indeed, we had nowhere to go!

At the graveside in Inverness I had been aware, in particular of two lovely Christian friends, Calum and Eileen Sutherland. I had not heard from them for a long time. They were husband and wife - the husband a Chartered Surveyor. They had come over to me and asked, 'Is there anything at all we can do?' Tearfully, I had muttered, 'If you hear of a small house for sale in Inverness, would you let me know, please?'

After returning to Edinburgh, the manse telephone was continually ringing with suggestions, ideas, costs and locations from these friends. I could not believe it possible that they had really meant what they said. They were marvellous - even driving to Edinburgh and taking Dawn and I out to dinner to get a clearer picture of what I would be able to afford.

By this time I had made several visits to the Department of Ministry and Mission of the Church of Scotland who advised me if possible to buy a small, modest house and they would authorise a loan at 1% interest. Thankfully, houses in Inverness were cheaper than in Edinburgh and our friends continued to search for us. A further phone call explained that a Scottish Special house particularly for disabled people was on the market and they asked us if we would make a day trip to Inverness to view it.

Dawn and I travelled by train and were met and taken to view the house in a terrific thunderstorm. As the rain battered the windows outside we looked around seeing that it appeared ideally suited to the two of us, especially as it contained a small, downstairs toilet. I was very badly crippled and using sticks, like Dawn.

We returned to Edinburgh. Our friends supplied us with food for the return journey and agreed to deal with the purchase of this house for us. The endless trouble these folk took on our behalf was marvellous. The householder was aiming for the highest bid, but our friends chased him around the Highlands until they found him and challenged him to draw the deal to a close, or our offer would be withdrawn. The owner accepted. Again the Lord provided and used two of his servants to deal with this great task which we could never have completed on our behalf. What compassion - what love and concern. We cannot repay such kindness, but the Lord will bless them. James 2: 14-20 states so clearly the test of good works. Dawn and I experienced the practice of this from the time we met at the graveside to this day.

Diana and Antony supplied us with many useful things for the kitchen and they continue to pay our television license. We were so grateful for all these gifts and help, and acknowledge God as the bounteous giver. However indebted we are to others, we give him the praise and glory for meeting our needs over and above our expectations.

A newly converted lady had come to help me daily in the manse during Rex's illness and she pleaded with me to allow her to come until we moved away. She was wonderful - packing carefully and cleaning and would never ever accept a single penny from me. She said she did it out of love for the Lord and for us!

Once the little house was bought in Inverness and we were ready to leave I had no desire to remain in the manse longer than necessary. A minister friend whose church was in the Borders, was a frequent visitor to us. He asked how Dawn and I were to be travelling to Inverness and when I said I would drive us up he was adamant in his refusal to allow me to do this. He insisted on driving us himself and returning the same day on the late train - more practical Christian help.

For our departure, our friends in Inverness had organised a removal van to collect all our belongings and requested us not to arrive until after lunch the day following the removal van. We did not understand this but I was quite incapable of trying to change whatever was happening so Dawn and I booked in to a Bed and Breakfast after driving north and we waited to be collected the following day.

We were called for and taken to our little house. Dawn and I could hardly believe what met our eyes. The house had been decorated, carpeted, curtains hung at all the windows and even a telephone installed upstairs. The furniture had been moved in, the china unpacked and even food put into the fridge.

What does one say or do? Several from the Inverness Church had helped and also a member of our friends' family. I will never forget the overwhelming Christian love and compassion which prompted this couple in particular and other friends to help us so much in our darkest days of sorrow and grief.

Before leaving for Edinburgh, Rex and I had regularly walked with our two dogs along the River Ness and around Bught Park. A few weeks after Dawn and I had settled into our home, I drove over to the same places and walked with our one remaining dog. The park was deserted and I sat on a park bench. As I sat there a strong feeling of tiredness and of release slowly came over me and I sobbed and sobbed - the deepest crying since the news of Rex's terminal illness. My heart was hurting and the tears came as rivers for a long time. I was glad nobody was there but I am sure God understood. I was not ashamed.

As I have said, grief affects people in different and unexpected ways. I will never cease to marvel at the strength the Lord gave to me during the months and weeks prior to Rex's death. I am not naturally a strong or stoical person. I had leaned on Rex particularly for so long but I believe that the Lord did transform me and take over, removing me from the depths into which I may otherwise have fallen.

Weeping releases but it also weakens. My sleep pattern had been disturbed for months and months, having to be always on the alert for Rex's needs. This time of weeping in Bught Park was to herald a beginning of a return to the rest and sleep which, I think, I badly needed.

Many Christians, including ministers, speak of the grief of a widow remaining for one year before the hurt and emptiness become less painful. They will only know how long it takes when they themselves have had to pass through such a time. A visitor once added, 'It is time that you rose above your grief.' I remember this as one of the most hurtful remarks. Nobody is able to predict how long grief should last.

Rather than dwell on this sort of advice which

widows like myself seem to so frequently receive, I prefer to think of a beautiful picture I have which my son drew for us. It is of a hand holding a person inside it, taking the idea from Isaiah 49: 15 and 16. It also contains a lovely verse which reads,

> Death hides, but it cannot divide;
> Thou art but on Christ's other side;
> Thou with Christ, Christ with me,
> And so together still are we.

It provides comfort which I find I often still need.

13
Beginning Again

And so Dawn and I began our new life in Inverness. We had received so much help from caring friends but now we had to settle in ourselves. Together we made the house comfortable and we set about trying to find a job for Dawn. As we had found previously, this was not an easy task, especially as we could not easily get into or about the town ourselves. Dawn always used two sticks and as I had become increasingly crippled with arthritis I too needed sticks in order to move: I shuffled around our kitchen leaning on the surfaces with my elbows. So dependent were we that Dawn and I called ourselves 'The Stick Brigade'.

As a widow I am much more fortunate than many women like myself in that I have Dawn with me. I am ever grateful for the love and companionship and joy with which she surrounds me. Unselfishly she had resigned her good job in Edinburgh and it was some time before we were able to find another in Inverness suitable for her. She did it out of love and I valued her closeness especially during those first months.

For I was discovering the ongoing pain of loneliness which all widows seem to know to one degree or another. Having been one of a partnership for many years and then to be separated was very traumatic and the repurcussions of this always seemed to make themselves felt. Perhaps they will always remain.

I was even made aware of my solitariness when I returned to the excellent evangelical church where we had worshipped before leaving for Edinburgh. For although we received great kindness from individual friends there I experienced an underlining of my solitary position when I attended the services. Entering the church alone, for Dawn was not with me, I took a seat in a pew. It seemed, however, that I had encroached upon the occupants' territory, daring to sit in the pew they had inhabited for years and they refused to move along to give me room: there would have been plenty of space but I was left hanging over the end of the seat into the aisle. I saw that my only chance of future comfort was to try an empty pew and there I sat. Nobody beckoned me or invited me to join them and I sat throughout the service alone.

It was such a simple thing and yet it hurt me deeply as I was already feeling so low. What a difference some friendliness or understanding would have made during those solitary Sunday services. Although I was aware that the purpose of going to church is to worship and glorify God, and certainly the teaching that we received could not be surpassed, perhaps a welcome to a newcomer would have made a great difference, enabling me to feel more able to participate in the subsequent proceedings.

My own common sense told me that there were many other suffering, lonely people there, widows and widowers, or other single people alone. I felt how different it could be if the Christian fellowship were conscious of how uplifting and helpful such thoughtfulness could be.

After Dawn settled into a new job in Inverness I began to find myself fretting to discover some activity with which to occupy my time. It was a situation I had not anticipated but after over fifty years of being fully occupied each day I should not really have been surprised. For I was suddenly in a position of uselessness which I was unused to and it only made me more aware that I no longer had Rex's wisdom and advice to which to turn.

Happily, however, I was soon able to rejoin two of the Bible Study and prayer groups which I had previously attended. The group of ladies which had met in Maurine Murchison's house had now grown to many groups around the town and I was asked if I would like to take over a group in our area whose present leader was leaving. This was God's loving and sympathetic care for me which helped to relieve the steady pain of grief in my heart and I welcomed the chance to use our new home, opening it up to those who were eager to gather around his holy book.

We began with four of us and this too grew over

the years until now, some years later, twelve gather every Wednesday morning in our small lounge. Together we meet as friends to study the Bible and share together how we should apply what is revealed to us in our lives. Six of us, however, have another bond which aids sympathy and understanding: we are all widows.

I also attended again an Overseas Missionary Fellowship prayer meeting. We had always maintained our contact with OMF, and writing to many members over the years had become part of our lives. Many of our correspondents had become our friends whom we had met up with during their furloughs - people like the Guinesses who had worked for many years in China and to whom Rex and I had been particularly close. Now I enjoyed this chance to become involved again and when the leader of the group later returned to work in Thailand, I began to hold the monthly meeting in our home. Dawn helped me and we were so glad to be able to use our home again in this way, allowing this fervent and concentrated prayer for missionaries to continue.

And so, as the months passed, with the help and concern of old and new friends and their assured prayers, I began to build my life again. It would be fruitless to recount the seemingly unending weariness and loneliness which the ongoing pain of my grief brought but suffice to say that the encouragement and compassion of these friends helped. I also knew that my Lord was dealing gently and quietly with me and his tender care was a great comfort. Often as Dawn and I shared our Bible readings and prayers together we knew him to be particularly close and I took heart.

About a year after we had arrived again in Inverness it became clear that a hip replacement operation was now necessary for me. It had been increasingly difficult for me to cope with running our little home and very hard for Dawn so I was admitted to hospital for surgery. My son,David came down from Orkney to be with me over the early days of surgery and immediately after.

One of the blessings about being unwell or in hospital is the lovely and sometimes unexpected visitors which one receives. As I lay drowsily on my bed one afternoon soon after my operation I saw an elderly couple walk into the centre of the ward. I looked - and I thought I must be in heaven! For these two people were our old friends who had been missionaries from China - Mary and Henry Guiness. How lovely it was to see them again. They were retired and lived just outside London and had taken advantage of a concession ticket from British Rail - £2 to travel anywhere in the country: for old age pensioners. These dear folk had prayed and felt that the Lord was telling them to go as far as possible. When they heard I was going into hospital they decided to travel all that distance to come and visit me! It was a wonderful reunion after a long separation.

My new hip was unbelievably super. The pain had gone and I was quickly learning to walk upright again. Within a few weeks I was able to throw away my sticks and I felt full of energy. The release from pain was so wonderful that I cannot praise the surgeons and staff enough.

Soon I was pronounced fit enough even to drive - if we only had a car! Our financial situation was such, however, that we could no longer afford one but I was concerned about Dawn. She is unable to use public transport and is restricted as to where she can go alone because of her lack of balance and dependence on her sticks. To be able to drive her as I had done in Edinburgh would, I felt, help Dawn - and relieve my mind!

A friend of mine was aware to a small degree of our situation and when she was at a function one evening she listened with particular interest to the speaker. He was a senior army officer and was explaining to the guests the work of The Officers Association Scottish Branch. When he mentioned that certain annuities were available to deserving widows, my friend thought of me and approached him afterwards to explain my situation. The outcome of this concern for our welfare was the granting of an annuity with which I am able to run a small car and I now can easily and independently transport us wherever we wish - yet another example of God's continuing provision for us in practical Christian help.

As a result of my operation and at the suggestion of this same friend of mine, I became involved in the Hospital League of Friends which visits patients in hospital giving companionship and comfort wherever possible. In particular, I visited the orthopaedic wards finding my experience with Rex and my own operation helpful in speaking to others.

Once I knocked on the door of a single room. The patient, I knew, was a lady waiting for a hip replacement. Having entered the room I introduced myself and explained the reason for my visit to which the lady in the bed, a woman of about my own age, replied haughtily that she did not require any visitors other than her family. She was not at all pleased at my 'intrusion'. I apologised and was about to leave when she stopped me. 'Wait,' she called, 'You have an English voice. Where do you come from? Why are you here?'

It is not often that my southern accent is of use here in the Highlands! As a result, however, of her noticing it we got into conversation and discovered that we had some things in common, particularly that we had both served in the army and we chatted for a long time. As I left I gave her a magazine and was invited to visit her again.

Following this lady's operation I visited her and this time was warmly greeted. It had transpired that the magazine I had left had made mention of the book of Joshua and had included some quotations. Nervous before her surgery she had been delighted with the message and had repeated the words 'be strong and of good courage' all the way to the operating theatre and said that I had been sent! In her time of fear and weakness she had known the need for strength and help which no surgeon or visitor could supply. This contact, with its difficult beginning, ended with her delightedly accepting a Daily Light, a book of bible verses and meditational passages, which she has since written to say she reads without fail morning and night and finds most helpful. It was so encouraging to be able to participate in opportunities like this which God provides.

Sometimes I have found it difficult to understand God's control of situations and I am aware that I often make mistakes. One such instance of this was when a new lady began to attend our growing Bible Study Group. She was a retired nursing sister, an intelligent woman with a real desire to discover more about what we believed. She, herself, was not a Christian but she asked endless questions and took away many books to read. We were so hopeful that she would come to know Jesus Christ that I read a note she left for me after one meeting with real excitement. It read, 'Thank you for everything, I have found what I want.' I called to visit her feeling very happy: I thought she had found Jesus.

What I discovered, to my dismay was that, instead, she had found the Jehovah's Witnesses - or more correctly, the Jehovah's Witnesses had found her! This lady had compared our little group to the members of this sect whom she found so loving and friendly and said she had found that many in our study group considered themselves superior and full of knowledge, making life so much more complicated than the one which she now embraced. She had also received two hours of instruction every week from her mentors and she refused to compare the Jehovah's Witnesses' version of the Bible with the Authorised Version which we used for our studies. Nothing would move her and I could only leave. We prayed very much that she would return but she has not done so yet. I felt very responsible that I had failed my Lord. I had been so wrong and struggle still to know his purpose in this difficult situation.

Partly I understood her need of friendliness. She is also a widow and has not even a family to be with her. Again I was reminded of my dear children who have given so much to me. Having moved house so often - nineteen times since my marriage - my roots are nowhere in particular. My real destination is with Christ but he has seen fit to give me my family until that time.

Diana is far away but we are in contact by phone. Dawn is my constant companion and my friend. Her own spirituality grows continually and her life is so different from the one she was consigned to at the age of seventeen. She has not been able to fulfill her earliest plans, except one perhaps. Dawn has a singing voice with which she loves to sing to her Lord. With a beautiful expression of the face which was for so long devoid of any emotion she brings joy to most who see her singing and she soon joined the choir in Inverness. Perhaps, therefore, she has finally become a 'church lady' which was her first ambition as a little girl!

David, with his wife, continues serving his Lord in the United Free Church ministry at present in

Northfield, Aberdeen. It always thrills me to hear him preaching. He is as bold and fearless for God as was his father. He is a constant, happy reminder to me of my beloved Rex. They are not so far away now and are always available at a moment's notice and to care for us should ever such circumstances arise.

And so our life in Inverness continues. Stepping forward for Christ must always be our priority and we pray that we can do so. In the army we had a phrase which was used to describe the change of stride of a marching company when they approached an obstacle, or perhaps a bridge. Marching across would perhaps damage a fragile structure so each would fall into his own stride to cross. Often that is just what I did with my early life - and went my own way! It also describes, however, how Jesus came into my life. To follow him I had to 'change step', change my stride, and in order to get to the other side I had to falteringly tread according to his instruction. 'Changing step' also gave the greatest reward, however - safety, a new and loving commander, a new army even, and a new path on which to march.

And Now...?

I am now past the Biblical years of three score and ten but perhaps it is still too soon to write my story for I am aware that God's blessings are still being graciously given to me. However, what I have written is what I so far have lived, mistakes and all! My mistakes were many but although I frequently broke out of line, out of step, before I was a Christian, becoming a Christian was much more revolutionary and radical than anything else I had ever done before and was not a mistake. For it meant an entirely new way of life.

There are those who have given themselves to Jesus when they are very young and have grown strong in the faith. I have found that some of them can be unaware that they are a little condescending to those converted later in life, almost questioning whether it is conversion or just a 'changed way of life'.

Surrendering to Jesus *is* a changed way of life! My lifestyle began to change from self-centredness, drinking, smoking, swearing and flirting when a backsliding, marvellous man married me, but I did not surrender to Jesus then. I listened, questioned, read and began to change my habits but it was not until I attended that house meeting that I became sure that knowing Jesus was the only way to change.

The young, or those converted in their youth, may not have experienced many of the sins which those converted in later years have committed and they cannot know how long it may take before the Holy Spirit gently leads one away from former habits and vices. I committed multitudes of sins not knowing them to be sinful, but just 'fun'. It takes time to confess as all these are brought to remembrance and to replace all the wrong, depending on the grace of God to make us more Christ-like!

Jesus knows the right time for each of us. Who are we to demand when, or how this should be? For me it has been a long process. Soon after becoming a Christian I was challenged by my friends because of my change: 'If you prefer a prayer meeting to playing bridge, so be it, but don't expect others to do the same. Keep this Jesus stuff to yourself!' But another said she felt able to remain friends with me because I wasn't so different - I still smoked and drank with her!

It would be wonderful if, irrespective of when the change occurs in our life we could work together. In some things old and young Christians are alike. I did not find Jesus. He was not lost! He found me as he finds us all and I am content that his timing was right.

As for the future, there is only one who can continue to help us change step with the world which does not know him and to keep in step with himself - Jesus. I pray that I may continue to do so in his strength.

I have found it difficult and emotionally upsetting to write this book, dreaming vividly of the past and reliving in my mind both distressing as well as happy incidents. Every day I have asked the Lord to guide my hand and to help me to write only that which would bring pleasure and glory to himself. Educationally, I am quite unqualified to write having left school before I was fourteen but the opportunities for travel, meeting so many people and encountering new cultures have helped to compensate I believe, for this lack of early schooling. I do not, however, pretend to be a writer and I humbly ask those who read this story to see in it my Maker who formed me once as a baby but who also remoulded and remade me, sometimes through suffering but always with his wisdom. If he has used me, even me, then I am grateful.

Editing and proofreading work for
Changing Step
was done by
Sheana Brown
11 Richmond Terrace
Aberdeen
AB2 4RP

Preaching Priest

An interesting biography of Martin Boos, a devoted servant of Christ. Boos was converted in the Roman Catholic Church and the story describes the many conflicts he had with church authorities as he persisted in preaching the true gospel.

192pp ISBN 1 871676 088 pocket paperback

Mussels At Midnight

The story of Stephen Anderson contains enough excitement and variety for two lifetimes. From dancing with the Queen to playing polo in the Egyptian desert; from a farm in Perthshire to the churches in Scotland. Stephen Anderson has been a captain in the army, a ski instructor, but above all a communicator of the gospel.

160 pp ISBN 0 906731 933 pocket paperback

To be published in 1991

Out Of The Tiger's Mouth

Dramatic escapes from the Chinese authorities were a feature of Charles Chao's early life. Not that he was a criminal; just a man determined to follow his Lord and Master whatever the risks and sacrifices as he developed the work of the Reformation Translation Fellowship.

160pp ISBN 1 871676 59 2 pocket paperback

The Only Way To Walk

The life of James Brown is a testimony to God's power and love. A dreadful accident in his ice-making plant left him without his legs, yet he has fought back to live a normal life and to testify that God is in control.

128pp ISBN 1 871676 43 6 pocket paperback